A PLAY THERAPY PRIMER

Therapeutic Approaches to Children with Emotional Problems

A PLAY THERAPY PRIMER

Therapeutic Approaches to Children with Emotional Problems

Vita Krall, Ph.D.

HUMAN SCIENCES PRESS, INC.

Library of Congress Cataloging in Publication Data

Krall, Vita.

A play therapy primer: therapeutic approaches to children with emotional problems / Vita Krall.

p. cm.

Includes bibliographies and index.

ISBN 0-89885-477-6

1. Play therapy. 2. Mentally ill children—Treatment. I. Title.

[DNLM: 1. Mental Disorders—in infancy & childhood. 2. Play Therapy—in infancy & childhood. WS 350.2 K885p]

RJ505.P6K73 1989

618.92′891653—dc20

DNLM/DLC 89-15512

for Library of Congress CIP

A Subsidiary of Plenum Publishing Corporation
233 Spring Street, New York, N.Y. 10013

Printed in the United States of America

To the parents and children

PREFACE

After the completion of the book *Developmental Psychodiagnostic Assessment of Children and Adolescents*, which describes the process of evaluation of child and adolescent emotional problems from severe to mild, it seemed necessary to go further. Once we have some understanding of the etiology and nature of the emotional condition of these patients, how then may we treat them?

I have long believed that verbal therapies were insufficient and often inappropriate to the treatment of many emotional conditions of childhood and adolescence. They presume the development and advance to secondary process thinking and a more developmentally advanced emotional condition than many of these children present. This issue is best understood when we speak of those autistic children who are without verbal abilities or speech. It is less understood for children who present with language. Children with language do not necessarily have the capacity for secondary process thinking, that is, abstract thought, or relational thought required for understanding interpretations of symbolic and indirect communications of unconscious blocks. Even here, we are speaking of the highest level of emotional disorder, neurosis, where the unconscious expresses itself through indirect and symbolic derivatives.

The more severe emotional conditions of childhood and adolescence have not progressed to this point in development. For the most severe, their condition is at the level of preverbal, sensorimotor, and primary process thinking: autism and childhood psychosis and the more severe borderline psychotic conditions. The character-disordered child also has not developed the capacity to bind and internalize anxiety to the extent that he has available to himself secondary process thinking. Unconscious impulses are acted out, and he has less use of secondary defenses. Verbal explanation is not understood by him, and interpretations are rejected during the early stages of treatment.

How then can we understand the emotional concerns of these youngsters, and how can we communicate with them? Play has often been called the language of childhood and/or the free associations of analysis. Since these children are at a nonverbal sensorimotor level in development, we can understand them through their nonverbal communications in play, and we can communicate with them through interpretation of their play. For the more severe conditions of psychosis (autism and symbiotic psychosis and the more severe borderline conditions), the play is initially used to build ego functions and to develop ego structures. As they move to more secondary process thinking in therapy, the interpretations can also move to a more verbal level.

This book demonstrates the use of play to both understand and communicate in the process of play therapy for the different levels of developmental disorder in childhood and adolescence. To better explain the process of play therapy with the various developmental disorders, at least one case example is included for each type of disorder.

We begin with a description of materials to be used in the play, the role of the therapist in the interaction, and the interpretation of play. Since the parent is so essential to the treatment of children, there is some discussion of the treatment of the parents. The developmental disorders that are covered are autistic and symbiotic psychosis, borderline disorders, narcissistic personality disorders, and neurosis. The book concludes with a discussion of termination issues.

Vita Krall

Milford, Connecticut

ACKNOWLEDGMENTS

To the staff and students of Michael Reese Hospital who gave support to this project.

CONTENTS

1

INTRODUCTION

This handbook introduces beginning students to the practice of play therapy. Play therapy is the therapy of choice for younger children.It is particularly useful for older latency-age children whose developmental arrests are at the preoedipal, preverbal, and action-oriented levels.

Play has existed as long as there have been children, and the theories of play have abounded from pre-exercise, to mastery, to recapitulation, to catharsis (Piaget, 1962). I prefer to use an integration of developmental and psychoanalytic theory to understand the play productions of children.

If we think of play as representing another form of intelligence, we can look at play within the same context as the development of thought and intelligence. Piaget (1962) differentiated the development of schemas (circular circuits) that form the basis for intelligent action, on the basis of assimilation to the ego, followed by accommodation of the ego to reality. In its simplest form, the simple reflex gives rise to reproductive assimilation by incorporating external elements into the reflex schema.

These later may become differentiated circular reactions. When the object provides an external stimulus recognized by the child in his assimilating activity, there is accommodation to the object beyond perception. Intelligent thought seeks a balance between assimilation and accommodation. According to Piaget, play subordinates accommodation to assimilation, being mainly concerned with needs satisfaction.

Play parallels the stages of intellectual development, from egocentricism, sensorimotor, and concrete operational thought, to formal logic, as well as in its development from practice play toward symbolism and symbolic play. Symbolic play mirrors the intellectual stages and structure of intelligence. "Moreover, the most adapted and most logical thought of which the young child is capable is still prelogical and egocentric, its structure being intermediate between the symbolic thought of play and adult thought" (Piaget, 1962). Piaget described symbolic play as one form of thought, the aim of which is to satisfy the ego. It is both conscious and unconscious, with an affective component of affective schemas that may be opposed to one another. Childhood memory is related to the primitive level of the intelligence of the young child. Unconscious symbolism, that which is unaware to the ego, he saw as more broad than repression per se. Piaget deviated from psychoanalytic theory in the belief that the addition of the concept of a conscious censor is unnecessary. He reversed the process. The censor is the expression of the unknown nature of the symbol. The symbol is itself the result of an early attempt at comprehension. The child's symbolic play runs the gamut from that which is entirely comprehensible to that which is not. A symbol is repressed and/or unconscious, when it is not in contact with reality because of its incompatibility with other tendencies in stable schema, including incompatible affective schemas. These concepts are highly congruent with the psychoanalytic concepts of conflict and repression.

Melanie Klein is the greatest proponent of the use of symbolic play of the child "to gain access to and liberate his phantasy" (Klein, 1948). Because anxiety interferes with verbal expression, play is used to gain direct access to the child's unconscious (Klein, 1948). Her opinion is that the unconscious of the child is peopled by symbols as it is not in adults. Here she split early from Anna Freud (1947), who thought that the child was too closely related to the reality of parental figures and that play is more expressive of the experiences of daily life. Anna Freud also criticized play as a form of free association, since the child lacks the motivation of the adult in analysis to control conscious interferences with associations.

A more recent analytic therapist who follows the Anna Freud position sees play not as the equivalent of free association, but as an ego-derived behavior that serves more than one purpose in the therapy (Esman, 1983). Esman also focuses on the parents as a source of information (reality environment). However, play is also used to interpret conflict and to bring it within the conscious control of the child. This point of view is a modification of the Anna Freud position. It adds the recognition of the often limited verbal expression of the child at younger ages and their dependency on parental figures and strong resistances (defenses).

Play is a universal in children. Play has structure and form, content and symbolism; it mirrors graphically even within a single session the developmental shifts and variabilities of each child's emotional, perceptual and intellectual life. The interpretation of the play presented must take into account the age of the child, the intellectual and developmental level of the child, and the vicissitudes of the mother–child relationship and the family environment, to interpret the conscious to unconscious symbols.

To begin to understand the play of children, one must be acutely aware of the normative expectations for play and then distinguish play presentations that are out of synchrony. In his naturalistic observations, Piaget (1962) identified three stages of play: practice play, symbolic play, and games with rules. Practice games, the first to appear, occur in activities that are experienced for the mere pleasure of it. These occur when the child is preverbal and in the sensorimotor stage, reappearing when the child is attempting a new activity. Piaget extensively classified symbolic play into several categories: projection of symbolic schema onto new objects, projection of imitative schemas on to new objects, simple identification of one object with another, identification of the child's body with that of other people or objects, simple combinations, compensatory combinations (correcting reality), and liquidating combinations (reliving reality by repetition). From the age of 4 to 7, these symbolic games begin to lose their interest. There is then a more straightforward imitation of reality, with three characteristics: orderliness, exact imitation of reality, and collective symbolism, that is, games played with others, including role taking. Games with rules he placed between the ages of 7 and 11 (Piaget, 1962).

Recent research by Field, De Stefano, and Koewler (1982) replicates this age progression expectancy for play. The play sequence for 20 months through 4 years of age was reality play, object fantasy, and person fantasy.

Field and co-workers relate this progression to cognitive maturity in symbolic activity to explain the progression from object to person fantasy and to increasing ability to plan and to verbalize plans. They found gender-related differences. The girls engaged in verbal interactions, positive interactions, person fantasy, and announced fantasy play a greater proportion of the time than boys. Boys spent more time in object fantasy.

Gondor (1964) described the sequence of fantasy in child psychotherapy as moving from a preoccupation with inanimate objects to animals, and then to human beings. Sarnoff (1976) traced the development of fantasy in early latency-age children as moving from amorphous monsters to figures that resemble people. Monsters and ghosts change into witches and robbers. Preadolescent fantasy is more preoccupied with the real objects in their lives. These progressions mirror the development of self and identifications, and the complexity of intellectual development from sensorimotor and concrete relationships to objects to person permanence and the internalized libidinal object (Mahler, 1967).

The nature of play materials and the manner in which they are presented may also have an impact on the type of play produced by the child. The Sears studies of doll play sparked a number of studies with interesting results, that are relevant. Using a modified and standardized dollhouse presentation, and varying some features of the dollhouse (e.g., standard doll family, realistic versus nonrealistic features), a number of findings emerged that facilitated decisions about the play setting. Phillips (1945) found that when play materials were of high realism, as opposed to low realism, there was more exploration of the toy materials when they were of high realism, and more organizational play when the materials were of low realism. There were also more changes in play thema and less continuity with low realism.

In lower socioeconomic class 3½-year-old preschool children, McLoyd (1983) found that high-structured toys elicit more noninteractive pretend play than do low-structured objects. There is also a gender-related difference, in that boys engaged in more fantastic themes and girls in more domestic themes. There seems to be some evidence that by this age, there is an interest in the environment that is being replicated, with the boys resonating to the climate of superheroes in the media, the girls showing a domestic interest. This mirrors the boys' greater physical activity at this age.

Pulaski (1976) differed with these findings. He reported that by the age of 5, the structure of the toys makes very little difference. He stated that high-fantasy children are already more imaginative than are low-fantasy children, whose play is much more closely related to their daily lives.

Children using a duplicate doll family versus a standard doll family in Robinson's study (1946) were more inhibited in identifying with the characters when they were duplicates of their own family, tending to reject socially unacceptable behavior. Pintler (1945) found that thematic aggression was reliably greater when there was high experimenter–child interaction. It began earlier in the sessions, and there was often more unusual play. Length of session was investigated by Phillips (1945), who found more exploration and organizational activities for the three shorter 20-minute sessions. The longer 60-minute session produced more tangential behavior and was of less interest and more frustrating to the children.

The interpretation of affective and motivational systems in play productions presents special problems. When change in aggression occurs, it seems to be in the direction of increase from session to session. Latency (or time before the first aggressive act) decreases from play sessions 1–2 for certain children. Children high in aggression continue to be high, while those low in aggression might increase or decrease. Also, both Bach (1945) and Jeffre Isch (1952) found that children known in preschool to be weakly destructive showed the greater increases in aggressive fantasy in early sessions than did strongly destructive children. High-punishment groups showed less increase than did low-punishment groups. Accident-prone children showed more increase than did accident-free children (Krall, 1953). These variations make it difficult for us to interpret the aggressive behavior of any specific child during a single session. Our problem might be that we are not differentiating between aggressive drive and overt demonstration of aggressive behavior. We also need to indicate whether we are talking about the feeling or the action.

A useful formulation might be that the overt expression of aggression may be quantitatively related to:

1. The strength of the original drive
2. The amount of frustration of that drive
3. The amount of substitute behavior that is permitted to satisfy the primary drive
4. The avoidance reactions built up in response to expression of aggression or aggression anxiety
5. The slope of the gradient or the curve of the drive and its expression

The overt expression of the aggression may be related to the algebraic summation of the approach or aggressive drive and to the aggression anxiety, or avoidance drive, as related to their respective gradients. We can explain the greater and more rapid increases in aggression for the weak destructive groups on the basis of a steeper avoidance gradient, predicting that inhibition to the expression of aggression will decrease more sharply in a permissive situation than will the expression of the aggression. Thus, there would be more change in the expression of overt aggression in the inhibited groups than in the normally and strongly aggressive groups of children. Here, the gradient may not be so steep, and the latter groups thus may have less need to maintain as vigilant internal or external controls over its expression.

The problem then is how to predict the amount of aggression from a single play session. When there is little aggression, do we have a normal child with little aggression, or do we have an inhibited child? Other aspects of play then have to be studied. Some of the features that have been studied have been the use of displacements and projections from same-sex dolls to others and the objects of the aggression. One then needs to know the hierarchy of displacement for each child to understand whether the child is displacing aggression from child doll to parent doll or demonstrating a real event. There are general findings suggesting that displacements for low-punished children are from self toward equipment. Medium-punished children showed parent dolls expressing the aggression. High-punished children showed the aggression being expressed by child doll agents (Sears, 1951). It is within the context and the consistency of any one child's expression that one may then look for the internal validity of ones inferences.

One hypothesis about the object of aggression might be that it would be the individual who is the most the source of the conflict, and/or it will be the parent, who is the most frequent frustrating object. The degree of inhibition related to aggression anxiety will determine the degree of displacement. Gewirtz (1950) found that older children, and Sac and Fox Indian girls showed more displacement of aggression, suggesting confirmation of this notion.

Another variable in the expression of aggression is whether it will be verbal or in action. It is a consistent finding that girls exhibit more verbal aggression than boys, who express more action aggression. The girls in Sears's (1951) material more often tended to scold, boss, and complain. A socialization and anxiety hypothesis would seem to account for these findings, with socialization anxiety appearing relevant to the sex and age differences that have been found.

The expression of intensity of aggression and the unusual forms of aggressive play seen in young children's play also warrant some comment. Here there may also be a hierarchy of symbols from weak to strong aggression, from saying "no" to the mother doll, to frying the mother doll on the stove or stuffing her down the toilet. Gondor (1964) pointed out the relationship of bizarre content and distortions to weak and fluctuating ego boundaries. I found the more peculiar types of doll play acts in severely accident-prone children (Krall, 1953).

Another approach to understanding the meaning of any specific act in a play setting would be to study the evidences of inhibition themselves. These would be denials, inhibited movements, escape, attack on objects, self warnings, refusal to cooperate, "play disruption"

(Erikson, 1964), self-punishment, restitution, doing and undoing, and self-defense (Levy, 1937).

A further issue that needs to be addressed in the understanding of children's play is whether the play is reproductive of or representative of the reality of the child. Analytic writers have emphasized the wish-fulfillment aspect of play, as well as the importance of repetition compulsion in explaining the perseveration of unpleasant or traumatic themes in play (Walder, 1976), or even what might seem to be minor happenings to adults (Erikson, 1964). Jeffre-Isch (1952) found children of highly rejecting and highly directive mothers to represent mother figures in doll play in this manner and to be recipients of much aggression and direction. However, these children are often more extreme in their fantasy play than in real life, interpreted to mean that some of their behavior might also be explained on the basis of wish fulfillment. It could also suggest that certain experiences take on more importance to the child than to the adult. Lerner and Murphy (1941) suggested the importance for clinical study of play protocols and the use of external evidence from the reality situation to understand and explain the play behaviors. One may combine this external evidence with internal evidence of repeated symbols, combined with measures of anxiety indicators.

Another source of data might be measures that have been found to co-vary together, such as dependency (giving and seeking of affection) and aggression. Highly aggressive children who are interpreted to have little affection at home also tend to demonstrate more affectionate and seeking of affection behavior in doll play. Children who are less aggressive display less affection and seeking of affection in doll play and are considered to have been less frustrated in affection attainment (Jeffre-Isch, 1952).

The most important source of information for interpretation of play therapy, however, is the type of relationship the child establishes with the therapist. Choice of materials and the sequence of play activities and occurrences are also of importance in interpretation. These characteristics of play therapy are addressed in later chapters.

2

CHOICE OF MATERIALS

The choice of toys to gain access to the child's inner and outer world may vary some with theoretical orientation; it also varies with the play environment that is available. Melanie Klein (1964) listed

> Little wooden men and women, usually in two sizes; cars; wheel-barrows, swings, trains; airplanes; animals; trees; bricks; houses; fences; paper; scissors; a not too sharp knife, pencils; chalks or paints; glue; balls and marbles; plasticene; and string.

Another pioneer, Virginia Axeline (1947), listed

> Nursing bottles; a doll family; a doll house with house materials including table, chairs, cot, doll bed, stove, tin dishes, pans, spoons, doll clothes, clothesline, clothespins, and clothes basket; a didee doll; a large rag doll; puppets; a puppet screen; crayons; clay, finger paints; sand; water; toy guns; peg-pounding sets; wooden mallet; paper dolls; little cars; airplanes; a table; an easel; an enamel-top table for finger painting and clay work; toy telephone; shelves, basin; small broom; mop; rags; drawing paper; finger-painting paper; old newspapers; inexpensive cutting paper; pictures of people, houses, animals, and other objects; and empty berry baskets to smash.

Checker games and mechanical toys are not suggested.

Esman (1983) recommended

> A good stock of paper for drawing and cutting; crayons and marking pens; plasticene or Play-Doh for modeling; blocks of various sizes (small and large) for building; small, flexible family dolls and a few pieces of doll furniture; a few hand puppets for dramatic play; a toy nursing bottle and a doll that can be dressed and undressed; a few cars and trucks; two toy guns; and a soft rubber or plastic ball. For latency age children, boys especially, a checker and chess set...and a set of plastic cowboys and Indians....

I have felt the need to orient myself with this plethora of suggestions. One research group has studied the actual toy preferences of children between the ages of 2 and 12 and found that the highest-ranking toys combining popularity, communication value, fantasy stimulation, and dynamic spread to be doll family, soldiers, gun, clay, paper and crayons, animals, planes, Nok-Out Bench, and trucks. These workers felt, however, that categories of toys are not nearly as important as a consideration of the possibilities of any particular toy that can be found in the general store (Beiser, 1976).

My own approach to this problem has been to think of toys from a psychodynamic framework. I am interested in toys that will elicit the widest array of structural, perceptual, intellectual, and symbolic play in the shortest amount of time. With a psychodynamic framework in mind, the many toys named above that are at times quite repetitive can be classified as follows:

Family toys: dolls, dollhouse, people puppets, soldiers
Representational toys: cars, boats, planes, trucks
Expressive toys: paper, paints, crayons, marking pencils
Sensory toys: clay, Play-Doh, plasticene
Structured materials: building blocks, puzzles
Motor toys: balls, ring-toss, Nok-Out Bench

Dependency toys (fuzzy toys): animals, puppet animals

Aggression toys: aggressive animals, Bozo the Clown, guns

Board games: range of games suitable for different developmental levels

The advantage to this classification is that it can be adapted to whatever space is available. For the school psychologist who has to travel to a number of schools carrying these materials, a selection can be made from the above categories, for example, a small set of dolls. The doll house can be omitted, except for a toy bed and a couple of chairs. A car or two, matchbox size, some paper and crayons, a stick of plasticene, and an aggressive animal can be included. An innovative school psychologist told me that she had asked the child to name something she should bring next week. All these materials can be carried in a shopping bag or in a folding dollhouse suitcase, which I designed some years ago (Krall, 1953).

The next level of space is often the corner of the therapist's office. Here a corner is set aside as the play corner, with toys on a shelf and a small table and chairs for painting and crayoning. The therapist's desk can be declared off limits and/or locked, or a screen can be set up to provide a more effective barrier for the play space.

If one has the luxury of a full playroom, the problem tends to be not space, but clutter. Over the years, working in play therapy with so many children with different interests, I have added to, rather than subtracted from my materials. This has its advantages in terms of making many choices available. Also, I have added some of my own artistic interests over the years, such as wood working and copper enameling. Some children are particularly helped with an opportunity to create and build something of their own. I have found, however, that it can be highly distracting, especially to either the younger child or the highly anxious child, or the hyperalert organically damaged child, to have too many stimuli in the room. In fact, one 3-year-old told me quite directly that I have "too many toys," and indeed I do. For choice of toy to be a meaningful clue, one needs occasionally to straighten out the room, classify contents, and eliminate some of the clutter, that is, make some choices.

3

THERAPIST AS SELF-OBJECT

Anna Freud's criticism of play as a tool for understanding the symbolism of child's play is that the child is not conscious of a need to work or of a need to give up conscious control over play as in true free associations (A. Freud, 1947). Clinicians today strongly recognize the need to alert the child being brought for examination and therapy immediately to the purpose for being there. This needs to be done whether or not the family has been able to explain the purpose to the child. Sometimes the family has threatened the child with the examination as a punishment. In some cases, I have known of children being deprived of food until they have complied with the examination. The child needs to understand immediately that there is a problem that is making someone, including themselves, unhappy, and that the therapist's purpose is to understand how and why this is so. The child can be told that he will be understood either from his words or his actions or play. If a child is in pain, the offer of help is understood. The child may not be able to express himself or herself in positive terms. Even negative, provocative, or oppositional behavior is a communication to the therapist.

Beyond this introduction, I add very little in the way of structure. Limits are handled more as they come up in the therapeutic contact, except for the general rule that they can do or say anything, except hurt themselves or the therapist. The major structure is the time of the meeting and the length of the session, with a time warning 5 or so minutes before the end of the session. Parents are told of the confidentiality of the meetings, as are the children. We talk more of the parents' role (and often attempts to invade the confidentiality) when we discuss work with the parents in Chapter 5.

The therapeutic process begins with the first contact with the parent(s) and with whatever explanation they have given to the child. The child is motivated to reveal himself (or not to reveal himself) with these preparations. Given the tools of the playroom and the therapist, the child will be stimulated to demonstrate through his total organism that which he wishes to communicate. He may communicate as much by what he does not do, as with what he does do. If there is no play disruption, he may reveal both his inner and outer world and, through his relationship with the therapist, his emotional–social level of development.

The relationship set up by the child with the therapist is the most revealing of diagnostic clues for the therapist at the beginning of the therapeutic process. It is also the major tool of the treatment. The words and actions of the child are the means by which the therapist understands the child's communications. However, it is through the relationship that there is therapeutic understanding. With the understanding of this relationship and the materials of the play and verbalizations, the therapist may understand the direction that treatment takes. In general, I allow the child to take the lead in initiating the relationship and in developing the process of therapy. The therapist follows, understands, responds to, and facilitates what I see as a dynamic process. I believe that a meeting with a child is a "happening" and I allow it to "happen."

The therapist offers himself/herself as a self object to whom the child can relate or organize him/herself around. It is the nature of the relationship set up that often offers the first clues as to the developmental level, that is, the level of object relations, and the nature of the child's pathology. We can expect the autistic child to remain aloof and to treat the therapist as another object in the room, probably ignoring the therapist, except as needed to overcome some obstacle in the environment. Psychotic children are more clingy, and one has the feeling of merger with them. One often has a feeling of intrusiveness from them, as well as great fatigue after the session. The play they engage in may be highly idiosyncratic, and the fantasy may or may not include the therapist. Boundaries between them and the therapist may be quite blurred. The disorganization of the psychosis may express itself in all behavior, including language and thought.

The largest group of children seen at present are the borderline and narcissistically damaged children. Most of these children come to the clinic with symptoms of conduct disturbance and/or behavior disorders at home and at school, with learning failure often as the referral problem. The more severely borderline group relate with a combination of closeness and distance and with splitting into bad and good objects and self. However, they may also be very clingy and needy of reassurance by the therapist.

Often, borderline children who are more idiosyncratic and overtly disturbed in the school or home environment may relate in a needy, more ingratiating and clingy fashion in a one-to-one relationship with a therapist. Language and thought may vary from intactness to disorganization, as will the play. There may be a metaphoric quality to their play.

Narcissistic children relate very quickly in the sessions and may want immediate gratification and materialistic evidence of the therapist's interest and admiration of their products or themselves. The quick relatedness is suggestive of interchangeability of objects without reciprocity, except as a need to be liked or to ingratiate. Play is for need gratification, not necessarily communication, and pleasure is the goal.

These children may express aggressive need systems very quickly, along with fears of loss and abandonment and separation anxiety. They may, however, be less likely to be conflicted over expressions of aggression or to show anxiety about the expressions of aggression. Some of these children come to the session with less ability to use the therapist as a need-gratifying object and, because of lack of trust and confidence in the environment, they relate to the examiners as to others, with hostility and oppositionality.

The neurotic child presents most similarly to our usual understanding of presentation of unconscious conflict, with the usual array of defensive and symbolic communications. The object relationship is more reciprocal and related, with appropriate distance, to a "new friend."

If we think of childhood psychopathology as occurring along this continuum from autism to psychosis, and then to the borderline and narcissistic disorders, and finally to neurosis and normality, we must expect that the child's mode of relatedness as described above will lead to a certain use of the therapist in the therapy. The use of the therapist as transference and self object will shift in the therapeutic process. Anna Freud thought of the child as not having a transference, as the parents are alive and well. However, one certainly does not have to hedge in stating that children will have some sort of relationship or lack of relationship that will mirror the relationships they have with significant others in their lives.

This will be the major force in the therapy. For the autistic child, the therapeutic task is to develop the relatedness. In behavioral approaches, the therapist provides a reward for eye contact (Kozloff, 1973). In structural therapy, intrusive methods are used (Des-Lauriers and Carlson, 1969). In more psychodynamically oriented therapies with autistic children, the therapist may use a combination of intrusiveness with affect and interpretations to make the child aware of the therapist. The goal is to attain the symbiotic relationship from which the child can individuate and separate. This can be done with few or simple materials, but for a long while the therapy may be largely nonverbal.

The goal for the symbiotically psychotic child is to transfer the unhealthy symbiosis with the parent to the therapist, again from which the child can then be helped to separate and individuate. This therapy can be done with some verbal help from the child and with interpretation of symbol and metaphor on the part of the therapist. Borderline treatment is an extension of this, with more fantasy material and metaphor available for interpretation. However, the therapist must be prepared for certain borderline aspects of personality during the therapeutic process. The borderline child slips often from reality-oriented levels to times of regression. The therapist must remain with the child in those periods of regression for the child to feel understood and for his defenses to be respected. The therapist must be prepared for splitting into good and bad object, and for the child to split into good and bad self. These aspects of the relationship can be understood and the child moved toward incorporating this understanding within himself for the development of a more cohesive sense of self. These therapies take a long time, and often the therapist becomes unsure as to what he is doing as the child perseverates over what seems to be the same themes over and over again. However, the quality of relatedness and interest in returning to tell the story can be the gauge for the therapist as to the solidity of the treatment work. Much of the work with these children concerns their issues with separation, loss, and abandonment. It is through and with the relationship with the therapist that they work out these issues.

Therapy with character-problem children begins at a later developmental level, although the issues are most often preoedipal. Character-problem children often act out their issues within the context of a therapeutic relationship. Unlike the neurotic child, who can relate reciprocally to the therapist and work more overtly on conflict and anxiety-related issues through verbalization and play, the character-disordered child literally acts out his issues in the therapeutic relationship. Thus, the child with control and oppositional issues acts controlling and oppositionally. The child with severe deprivation and loss and abandonment issues acts out his neediness and lack of trust that he will be abandoned. He may use lots of materials, but it is the use to which he puts the materials to communicate to the therapist his character and relationship problems that is the focus. The more recent grasp and understanding of this level of development has been described by the various proponents of self psychology (Kohut, 1983). These children have experienced severe emotional deprivations, either real or perceived, and have suffered narcissistic injury, low self-esteem, narcissistic rage reaction, and subsequent depression. They often act this out in masked depression and depressive equivalents. It is often the behavioral reaction that we see, and not the depression. They continue this behavior with the therapist. The materials are the mode through which they communicate this hurt and depression. The therapy provides a safe place to communicate these feelings and experiences. The grandiosity and omnipotent defenses that overlay the helplessness and vulnerability feelings have to be worked through in the therapy. Corrective experiences can then be fostered and, from them, object relations and reciprocity can be developed within a context of love and trust.

The therapy most often thought of is the treatment of children with neurotic or neurotic behavior problems. These children are rarer now because of the cultural move toward overpermissiveness and overindulgence, without the development of reciprocity or frustration tolerance. The methods are more tried and true when there is a true neurosis: the unraveling of defense toward understanding of conflict and reduction of anxiety. These children are probably our most verbal, with the best observing egos. They can be taught to observe when they have not characteristically done so. They already have reciprocal relationships. The level of development has more truly reached or gone beyond an oedipal level, and they are capable of more than dyadic relationships. The problem is not primarily in development of relationship, or of separation and individuation. It is not their object relationships that are at fault, or their sense of self. There may be a conflict of moral values that have been incorporated from within, and they have both the reflective power and the ego strength to explore those issues. Thus, play can be used to act out the more unconscious motives and conflicts. Verbalizations are more increasingly available to them.

4

INTERPRETATION OF PLAY

There has been much agreement across the variety of methods used, including free play, as to the components that form the basis of interpretation of play. One of the earliest play methods was developed by Charlotte Buhler (1949) and adapted by Margaret Lowenfeld (1970) and recently modified as the Sand Test (Aoki, 1981) and the Swedish Erica test (Sjolund, 1981). The method uses a sandbox in which the child is instructed to build a world from miniature construction toys (e.g., houses) and people and animals. These tests are then interpreted on the basis of the elements used and symptoms of aggression, emptiness, distortion, and rigidity. Aoki (1981) in Japan demonstrated that more adjusted children tended to change their productions in sand play, whereas delinquents and emotionally disturbed children persisted in very similar creations. He inferred that this was either because of the pressure of certain central issues for them or because of lack of flexibility.

The Erica method introduced in Sweden (Sjolund, 1981) interprets the sand play on the basis of choice of material. It involves a formal analysis that categorizes the level of structure from recognizing and naming, indifferent placement, sorting, configuration, juxtaposing, conventional groupings, meaningful wholes, chaotic groupings, bizarre groupings, and thematic analysis.

The Miniature Life Toy Situation presents similar materials without the sandbox (Murphy, 1956). The child is asked to play with construction and miniature play people to develop in the microcosm the macrocosm of his world. Interpretation is based on the toys chosen, space used, physical movements, affect, organization of the play, configurations and patterns of play, and content and thema of the play.

Howe and Silvern (1981) recently contributed some classifications of interpretation that are reliably measured from observations of free play therapy sessions. They have developed scales for Emotional Discomfort, Fantasy Play, Social Inadequacy, and Maladjustment. They found that defensiveness did not occur in sufficient amount to form a separate scale but seemed to be an aspect of the cognitive, social, and affective functioning.

Pelligrini (1982) has also developed a classification system for interpreting children's play. His classification is based on Piaget's categories of play and on Parten's classification of social play, combined with an analysis of speech development. Ratings of play along the continuum from functional, constructive, sociodramatic play to games with rules may be multiplied (ratings of 1–4) with ratings of levels of social play (Unoccupied behavior, solitary play, associative play, and cooperative play (ratings of 1–4) to yield a complexity score for the child's behavior. This may be combined with observing the child's speech—phonology, syntax, and semantics—

to determine the maturational level of speech usage. The complexity of play measure and level of speech development may then be a useful tool to assess the child's cognitive and maturational development.

A test of symbolic play (imaginative play) (Lowe & Costello, 1976) has also been validated (Udwin & Yule, 1982). This test reliably and validly discriminates between a language-delayed group and a normal control group of preschool boys in the dimension of imaginativeness in free play.

Summarizing and drawing on these investigations, I would suggest the following areas of exploration for the interpretation of play either in diagnosis or in therapy. Blatt (1975) indicated that the diagnostic session is, can be, and should be considered a therapeutic contact. I believe that each therapy session can be considered a diagnostic session in and of itself, and therapy can then be monitored.

Structural Aspects

The structural aspects of the child's play deals first with the use of the space provided and with how it is organized. Is there order or disorganization in the use of space? Are structures such as fences or objects used to make boundaries, and are there gaps in the boundaries? Is there clarity or confusion in the use of the space? Is the space disconnected or disarranged? Is it tightly enclosed or rigid, or is it open and fluid? We may then make some inferences about the controls and defenses from these observations, taking into account the types of chaos that those children may in reality be coming from in their homes.

Perception, Motility, and Cognition

The chronological age of the child may be a start at estimating developmental level and age expectancy for any particular child. This may not be sufficient. Sometimes a general evaluation gives the approximate intellectual level of the child. If this is absent, the play can be evaluated from a perceptual and cognitive point of view; it may also supplement the other evaluations. The child's ability to perceive and organize the play objects as well as his fine and large motor coordination can be observed. The ability to develop integrated and sequentially coherent fantasy can be evaluated for intellectual level, much as story thema from picture story tests are evaluated. Language and language structure can be observed for intactness of syntax, articulation, and approximation to standard English. It is important for the therapist to have knowledge of the reality situation and of whether standard English is spoken at home.

Content, Conflict, and Dynamics: Psychosexual Level of Conflict

The thema or context of the play may reveal the level of conflict from a psychosexual point of view. The age of the child is again important here, as the expectation for a particular level of development is important to remember in interpreting any specific thematic content. Early preschool play is often involved with feeding, bathing, and toileting, in the representation of everyday life. It may be the particular preoccupation with such an event and its repetition that may reveal its importance for any particular child. It may be the particular doll figures that are depicted in that situation and with the preceding and following sequences. For older children, remnants of previous psychosexual stages (oral, anal, phallic, oedipal, latency) may represent fixations or regressions that will be of particular importance in understanding the individual child's dynamics. The combination of preoccupations with specific conflict areas, with indicators of anxiety or defensiveness may help pinpoint the child's central areas of concern.

USE OF OBJECTS (PLAY MATERIALS)

The choice of play material, and the sequence of choice of material, becomes an important interpretative element. From the hierarchy of materials suggested earlier, with which does the child choose to start? How global or distant an object does he choose? At what psychosexual level is the choice of material? Does it represent material evoking phallic aggression or sensory dependency neediness? Is there a shift in sequence as the play progresses from distance objects to objects that express conflict? From objects to animals to people? Is the child freed by the end of the session to express direct affects with the toys, at the toys, or at the therapist? One can also look for flow and discontinuity. The discontinuity may express the interplay of conflict expression alternating with anxiety and defensiveness. One may then ask what preceded the inhibition and what followed the inhibition.

Sequence and Process

The interplay of the various aspects and levels of interpretation are studied throughout the play session in the sequence and process. It is of interest to note which objects are touched and in what order, that is, which objects lead to which. The general rhythm of this sequence is of importance in telling us where there is tension and anxiety, pointing to a central issue. The psychosexual level of the objects and the thema surrounding the use of the objects may be further revealing. At the same time, one needs to observe the involvement of the child with the therapist. How the child uses the object of the therapist, (in the sense described by Winnicott, 1975), becomes meaningful both in and of itself and in its relationship to the sequence of the play. Is the therapist used for affection, soothing, approval, or need gratification? Or is the therapist seen as frustrator? Or is the therapist responded to alternately in both ways, depending on the play action involved? Seemingly accidental physical actions can lead to an understanding of a central issue. For example, a toy drops or breaks, or there are "not enough" pieces, leading to disruption. Inhibition can mean conflict or incapacity. A sequence can be finished because it has said it all. The difference needs to be recognized.

Observation and Recording

The basic observational data are the play interactions, and the therapist must be a good observer. I encourage my students to reconstruct complete process notes following the session. The therapist can jot down physical actions and objects as they are played with, with the "he did, I did" and "he said, I said" added in later. The notes serve as a mnemonic device to remember and reconstruct the order of the session.

FIRST PRESENTATION

I consider the first contact with the child for the first session the first presentation. I assume that the child comes in pain, no matter how the session has been explained. I assume then that the child will communicate the central conflicts and issues in some graphic manner through play and interaction with the therapist during this first session. The interplay of the organizational aspect of the play and use of space, the choice of material and level of conflict, and the communicative value of content of theme within the context of the relationship with the therapist should yield some clues. It is also important not to neglect an isolated nonverbal message during the play: the choice of a symbol, the squeezing of the nose of a toy, an isolated nonverbal behavior that breaks through the repressive barrier. One looks for the symbolic communications and the varying levels of conscious and unconscious meanings of the behaviors. The child has a repetition–compulsion to reproduce behaviors and materials that relate to the central issues and conflicts. I have also noted in any therapy with a particular child that the themes of the first presentation are repeated and worked over many, many times during the course of any particular child's total treatment. It is as if the child condenses into that first session all the unconscious and conscious concerns that will be the subject of the total treatment, if the therapist could but be aware of these in the first instance. However, it takes a whole treatment course to unravel, understand, and bring into awareness these concerns.

5

PARENT AND CROSSOVER THERAPY

Parental cooperation and involvement, and at least cooperation from the parent of an adolescent, are necessary before treatment of a child can proceed. As Anna Freud (1947) pointed out, the child continues to live with the parental or surrogate figures, and a reality relationship with parental figures is present. In addition, the child is completely dependent on the child's parent(s) for transport to the treatment session, unless the child is old enough to travel alone. In the inner city, children can travel alone at a younger age, which is lucky for many of these children. When children become motivated to continue the treatment relationship, they often are the ones who come regularly to treatment, while the parent remains uninvolved.

The parents of adolescents should be involved at least in the diagnostic process. Adolescents are the most difficult to engage in the treatment process, when they are brought by a parent who identifies them as the problem. For this reason, the sooner the parent can be dissociated from the treatment process, the better. If the adolescent feels that his needs and wishes are being addressed, it may be possible to engage him in the treatment process. The parents of adolescents, as those of children, are quickly informed about the confidentiality of the patient's information. It is important to handle this issue diplomatically so as not to drive the parent to withdraw the adolescent from treatment. Parental intrusiveness into the treatment process is often one of the most difficult problems to handle with both children and adolescents. The form that this intrusiveness takes may be either to ask the patient or therapist what has transpired during a session or to tell the patient to tell the therapist something or to work on a particular problem during the session. When play or activities are used with the child or adolescent, another form that parental intrusiveness takes is complaints that their child says that he is only playing: Aren't you talking about my child's problems? How can just playing help? The patient may sense this and either deliberately expose that he is playing, in opposition to the parent. Or the younger child may expose this to ask for permission to play.

Parents often bring their child to treatment because they are annoyed or irritated with the child's behavior. One must be very careful not to overidentify with the child's pain in working with these parents at the beginning of the treatment process. Such an overidentification can drive these parents away in the belief that you have failed to realize how bad the child is. You need the parents to feel that you empathize with their pain as well and that you would like to understand so that you can ease the pain of all within the family.

Once the diagnostic process is completed, I like to see the parents about once a month to work with them on their issues. I am very flexible about how often and when these appointments are made. I make adjustments for the parents' work schedules and often make appointments on evenings and weekends, when necessary. I also am available by telephone. In some cases, this may become a treatment vehicle. In private practice, depending on the situation, one can charge for these telephone calls. This can legitimize the calls and ease the guilt about their frequency or length.

I approach the treatment of parents as I would a regular treatment with an adult. I do not see collateral treatment as an approach of a lesser choice or technique. Treatment of the parent or parents may begin with a focus on the child and the child's problems, but most often the process moves to both the personal issues of the single parent or to the marital issues of the parents in an intact family. Where both parents come to the session, I see them together, unless they request otherwise. I do not use a directive approach in the treatment of parents, and I follow their direction in terms of which issues they wish to address. My philosophy of the treatment of parents is that happier parents are better able to parent their children. This may seem to take us far afield from their direct relationship with the children. However, in easing their personal pain, they are more free to parent.

I have had parents come to me who were so conscientiously involved with their children that they had never been away from them overnight, on vacation, or even to go out to dinner alone. One particular parent pair were indeed suffering "battle fatigue." I often ask parents what they themselves are doing for personal enjoyment. It is as if this is a new idea for them. Encouraging such parents to take time for themselves relieves them of any guilt for spending time on themselves and reduces tension in the family. It also makes it less likely that parental resentment will continue to be focused on the identified patient. In fact, I often find that as the patient's treatment progresses, the parents begin to pay more attention to other children in the family. They also often begin to see that another child is provoking the identified patient and that they have been overlooking that other child's faults. It is important to realize that in some cases, a family system is at work that requires a child to be the displacement object for parental resentments; the parents may seek another displacement object in the family, as the identified patient improves.

In work with parents, I may deviate from more strict analytic rules. For example, in some instances I have shared a social occasion, such as going out to dinner, with a family. Usually, I have said we can do this after the treatment is over, and then the family later forgets all about this. In one instance, I remember that I did go out to dinner during the treatment. The guardians of the child were the grandparents, who had legal custody. The grandfather was a professional who needed very much to feel that his expertise and collegial level were being appreciated. On this occasion, I learned more about his personal history than I had during the initial diagnostic session. In another case, I agreed to help a professional parent learn one of the major personality instruments. One does have to watch that the relationship with parental figures does not get too closely personal. It is always a matter of one's own personal comfort in dealing with closeness and with the ability to retain boundaries in such a relationship. For example, with another family, when they requested family therapy, I suggested that they seek another therapist for this problem. They subsequently realized that they did not need family treatment. It appeared clear at this point that it had been a way of hanging onto the treatment relationship with me.

One needs continued parental cooperation in the treatment process. Children will refuse to come during periods of anger or pain. They will feign illness or delay preparations for coming to treatment so as to be late or miss the session altogether. When legitimate activities come up, such as a birthday party or prized outing at school, I rearrange appointments as much as possible or allow a missed session. However, I urge parents to insist on session regularity and attendance. This sometimes means the patient has to be carried to the car. I deal with the patient's anger or withdrawal when the patient arrives, with whatever the therapeutic meaning is at the time.

Sometimes during the course of a longer treatment process, we reach a stalemate in the treatment. The parent continues to complain of the child's behavior, and the child continues to complain of parental maltreatment. At these times, I may bring the parent and child together for some joint sessions, so that each can tell the other how they feel, in the interest of facilitating and fostering better communication. With the therapist remaining a neutral party, they may be able to give up some of their anger and come to understand each other better. This approach also has the benefit of interfering with the exaggerations that each have been making and of reducing attempts at manipulating and splitting the therapeutic relationship. Often the parent is jealous of the attention that the patient is getting from the therapist, and the joint meetings have the benefit of reducing this type of jealousy. The relationship is shifted back to parent and child.

I have also used joint meetings between a parent

and child when the parent has not been giving an older preadolescent enough freedom and independence. This gives the child an opportunity to ask for these opportunities with the backing of the therapist. It allows the parent to hear the patient better, and they can work out some of their separation and individuation issues together.

Another type of situation in which I have used joint sessions is when there are serious reality issues about which patient and parent are very stressed. One situation of this type was a foster parent who brought the foster child to treatment at the direction of a social agency. She was initially somewhat resentful of having to bring the foster child. Gradually, with joint sessions at the end of the patient's sessions, the foster mother came to appreciate the support of the therapist. She began to air her serious concerns as to whether she would be able to retain the child in her home. Her desire was to adopt the child, but relatives perceived as previously uninterested in the child were standing in the way of the adoption. Both the foster mother and the child needed considerable support for some time while the slow court processes evolved and during the times when the child was required by the court to make visitations to these relatives.

Another type of situation in which I may call for a joint meeting between parents and child is when the child appears to be better, but the parents are not recognizing this. This seemed to be the case with parents who requested family therapy at the end of treatment sessions with the child. This was a family of two professional parents, one of whom was considerably older than the other. There were differences between them having to do with discipline and more serious marital issues. They were profiting from the therapy with me and overlooking the real improvement in their child. The parents had begun to recognize that the younger sibling had been provoking some of the patient's behavior. They had therefore made the decision to terminate and to think about family therapy. The child patient then told his parents and me, during the termination session, that he was also at fault in the problems between him and his brother. The parents then decided that they did not need family therapy.

Many times I have tested or treated other children in the family once one child has completed treatment. During the course of treating children, where I have known the whole family, family sessions have been helpful in providing boundaries for these multiple treatments. I have also been asked for joint sessions when there have been serious emergencies and crises in the family system. This might involve a family move, a question of separate placement of one or more of the children, or serious illness of a parent.

Wilfred T. Miller (1982) called this method of treatment *crossover therapy*. He defines this as operative when "the therapist physically moves into and out of family system or dyad system and also joins with the child or adolescent in a private space, separate from the family or dyad." Miller recommends this approach to facilitate the child or adolescent's movement through a normal developmental phase within the family system. He suggests that it is particularly useful when the patient demonstrates readiness for growth that has been temporarily blocked. Miller claims that it can also be useful during an impasse in treatment or when the parent is overtly distrustful of a particular therapist. A major limitation is when there is a family secret that the child or adolescent is aware of that cannot be discussed during the family sessions, in which case the joint session might interfere with exploration during individual sessions. Miller believes that joint sessions can also interfere with separation and individuation from the family system. I have found that joint sessions can be helpful in this regard.

In one case I found joint sessions helpful to some extent at the time in clarifying communication issues. However, the mother's rigidity and height of expectations were such that indeed the child's feeling that she could never please her mother was substantiated in further work with both parent and child. The mother had been analyzed previously, and she came to some dramatic insights in her individual sessions with me. She explored some very painful memories regarding her own mother, father, and stepmother. She was even able to relate some of her rigid expectations to the need to live up to her own parents' expectations, as well as her fears of loss and abandonment. She seemed unable to translate these insights into her behavior with her own child. Toward the end of the child's treatment with me, the mother remarried for the third time. The new stepfather was amenable to suggestion and was also more reasonable in his demands. I suggested that perhaps the mother needed further treatment to work out some of the issues that had emerged in her contacts with me. She preferred to think of the patient as unreasonable, and probably myself as well. In this case, the joint sessions only served to heighten the tension between the child and mother and between mother and therapist. Without resolution of some of mother's deeper issues, it seemed that the treatment was at an impasse. I terminated the case at this point. The child continued to telephone me for support in her relationship with her mother. I redirected her to discuss her feelings with the mother after several of these phone calls. The mother later sought help for the child with another therapist, at the child's request.

Even with these difficult situations, joint sessions are often helpful to clarify and redirect therapeutic efforts. It was my impression that these sessions had a facilitating effect, in many of the cases, and in others they determined the next step for the family. Where termination was approaching, joint sessions offered an opportunity to review the course of treatment and a resolution of some of the transference issues. Joint sessions also facilitated the termination process and redirected the relationship of the patient back to the parents.

6

AUTISTIC AND SYMBIOTIC PSYCHOSIS

The three major approaches to treating autistic children are behavioral, intrusive, and psychodynamic relationship oriented. The behavioral approaches have been well publicized with claims of high percentage improvement by Lovaas (1987). Behavioral approaches are particularly helpful with children who are self-punitive in their behaviors. They have also been used to develop eye contact with these children and are important in developing self-help care and habits. Critics of the behavioral approaches alone are concerned with the automaticity of some of the changes with and the need for better development of affects.

The DesLauriers–Carlson approach of intrusive interventions was described in *Your Child Is Asleep* (1969). These methods were further expanded on by Jernberg in *Theraplay* (1979). The philosophical base to this approach has been to provide the infantile experiences with body boundaries missed by these children during early infancy. They also seek to intrude on the hypoactive autistic child's aloof world and to dampen the hyperactive autistic child's hyperalertness to stimuli. I have found this approach helpful in beginning the establishment of contact with the autistic child, but have gone on to add the more relationship, psychodynamically oriented approach in the later phases of treatment, as have DesLauriers and Carlson.

This chapter briefly describes an example of play therapy with the autistic child using first an intrusive approach and then a relationship-oriented approach, but with both approaches having a play orientation. C. was a 4-year-old when I first saw him from behind a one-way vision screen. He was having language stimulation with a speech therapist. At this time, he had no spontaneous speech. The speech therapist was in the process of saying the numbers of 1–10, and C. imitated the word "ten." I had been asked to observe him to see whether I thought I wanted to take him on in treatment. I decided that with his language imitation he might have a better prognosis than many autistic children without speech. It has been said that age 6 is the magic age for the development of speech in these children, and he was only 4 years of age.

I decided to begin with an intrusive approach to develop some relatedness and eye contact. Since some of the method uses swinging and other physical activities, I asked a male graduate student to be my co-therapist for the physical carrying and swinging that would be necessary. The play of autistic children most often involves a few objects that they move back and forth and/or line up obsessively. The play environment was very simple. To begin with, we had some small cars and a truck in the playroom; we also had a tall double tower of large cardboard blocks. We began by sitting down on the floor with C. To make him aware of us, we intervened in his play. He could no longer move the cars or truck about aimlessly. We arranged the play so that he had to include us, and he could no longer ignore us to continue his play. We ran the objects over to him; he was gradually directed to move them back to us. This game was repeated over and over, and later a ball was substituted for the cars and truck.

When C. became interested in piling the blocks to make the tower, he was lifted up by Bob to put the last block. Eventually, he would not be lifted unless he said "up." He was also swung and often carried about by Bob. We were developing some awareness of body boundaries. As relatedness began to develop and he knew who both of us were, we began to move into the more relationship therapy aspect of the treatment. During the second year, the first Bob left, and a second Bob took his place. C. seemed to accept this transition well, and the lack of name change might have helped in this regard.

We brought in a manual-type record changer, and we began to play Ella Jenkins records suitable for preschool age. C. sat on my lap for these activities and learned to change the records and to hum along with the music. We also had many preschool matching-type games, at which C. became very proficient. It seemed to us that C. was bright, but we were not getting any spontaneous speech. At home, he was an avid watcher of sports programs on TV, and he was enrolled in a residential day-treatment program that used behavioral approaches.

Two years into the twice-a-week therapy, his mother felt she was no longer able to take the hour-long trip on the train. She was in treatment with me, and she became phobic about riding the train. The mother, however, was able to separate from her own mother. She had been living with her family in her parents' home. She and father bought their own home and moved shortly after they terminated the treatment. The house had a large backyard with apple trees. Shortly after moving into the new house, C. saw the trees in the backyard and said his first spontaneous sentence, "I want to climb a tree." His speech came in sounding somewhat sing-song and with some articulation difficulties. It became apparent, when he began to speak, that he was indeed taking in the sports programs that he had been watching for so long on TV. He would focus on the game scores and the names of the players and could now report on these interests. I did see him several years later, but I have no other important follow-up on this case.

I will give a more detailed account of the play therapy with a child referred to us at age five years, eleven months from our Children's Hospital, as I have available to me the records of this case, and have complete follow-up on her. The final diagnosis on this girl was of childhood schizophrenia with a secondary autistic regression. It is my experience with our clinic population that we rarely see pure cases of early infantile autism. We more often see children with autism, moving into a symbiotic position, or symbiotic children with autistic features.

Case Example: M. M. was referred by her school after a few weeks in Head Start and a year in kindergarten. She was described as responding to questions by repeating what was said to her. When asked her name, she said, "anteater, lion, Jackie Mason." She used loud profanity, wandered around the room talking to herself, and did not communicate with anyone in the classroom. At that time, the school reported a mental age of three years, eight months and an IQ of 58 on the

Stanford–Binet Form L-M intelligence test, at age five years, eleven months.

The occupational therapist in the hospital described M. as continuously rising from her chair during her testing session of 2 hours' duration. She would gaze out the window or play with test objects or chairs in the room. At the window, which faces the city, she would say: "Look at the ocean, see all the fishes and Flipper and the dolphin." The therapist would purposely deny her description of the cityscape, and M. would disregard this and continue her fantasy. If the therapist could not understand her and asked her to repeat what she had said, M. could repeat her statement. Eye contact was seldom established, and the therapist elicited eye contact for approximately 1 minute by physically positioning M. and verbally commanding her to "look at me." M.'s reaction to this, about 15 minutes later, was to grab the therapist's ears tightly and, while shaking her vigorously, said, "look at me," etc. Questions were inappropriately answered. To, "What would you do if you lost something?," she answered, "I would put house slippers on baby and get in carriage and go to Los Angeles to have my hair cut." Question: "Who lives in the house with you?" Answer: "Flipper and dolphins," or later to the same question, "I would put my arm like this," with a demonstration of putting her stockings on and off repeatedly for about 3 minutes.

In a second session, there were more toys. She did not pay much attention to any specific toy, but the toys she played with were age appropriate, and she named the toys correctly (e.g., monkey, doll buggy, horses, cows, sheep, circus, elephant). She accompanied her play with conversation that included giving commands to herself or repeating something the therapist said. For example, she would say, "talk, look at me," "don't put that in there," or "I dropped it." Once she turned to the therapist to ask if a letter was an N or an M on the magnetic alphabet board.

M. is the third child in a sibship of three. She has two

older brothers. Her mother discovered she was pregnant after separating from M.'s father. The mother developed diabetes during this pregnancy, and the delivery was by cesarean section. The mother was rehospitalized for a fever until the baby was 12 days old; the mother poignantly described her feelings of isolation at having to look at M. through a glass at that time. Because of an abscess, breast feeding was given up at 2 months. M. sat at 6 months and walked at 18 months. At that time, M. was using words like "wa wa" for water. The major difficulty noted during her infancy was hospitalization for whooping cough at 8 months. M. did not seem to know her mother after this, and when her mother spanked one of the boys for something she slapped her mother's face. M. is described as having been less noisy after this, but a happy baby. She is described as having been an easy child to care for, and she seldom cried and was described as more controllable than her brothers. At age 2 or 3, she is described as having roamed around the house at night and getting into the refrigerator. She liked to play with her brothers' toys and did not become interested in dolls until older. Her mother did discipline her physically at first, but later found that showing her the strap was sufficient. M. was not allowed outside by herself because of the high-delinquency area they lived in, but her mother also described her as embarrassing to take outside with her. She would hit strangers and talk loudly. It was difficult to obtain an accurate description of M. from the mother, who did not see anything the matter with her. She came for evaluation on the school's insistence.

The full diagnostic evaluation in our clinic came 7 months later. M. was six years, seven months at the age of the psychological testing. She obtained a Harris–Goodenough standard score of 77 on the Draw A Person test, an M.A. of 3–10, and an IQ of 54 on the Stanford–Binet Form L-M Intelligence Test. Her test behavior was similar to that with the occupational therapist. Her attention could be held on nonverbal items, but on verbal items she would respond with unrelated material, or she repeated the question. She was better related in a second testing session and remembered my name. When I was helping her mother with the Rimland Behavior Disturbed Checklist, she initiated contact with me by asking me the colors of crayons. Eye contact was good, she spoke to me by name, and she obviously enjoyed the session.

The Rimland checklist describes M. as having been a normal-appearing infant. Her mother described no autistic behaviors, including preservation of sameness. She reached out and prepared herself to be picked up; she was cuddly and liked to be held. Some change in behavior was noted after the 10-day hospitalization for whooping cough. She was described as later rocking in her crib, having an unusually good memory, engaging at this time in rocking, looking through or walking through people, seeming to be in a shell, and sometimes whirling herself like a top. The mother described M. as hyperactive, constantly moving, and changing quickly from one thing to another. She first spoke at 1½ years of age, with about average pronunciation. At this time, she used the words I, yes, and no. There was no peculiar word usage that her mother could report. However, it was difficult to evaluate the mother's reports on the Rimland checklist, since she did not consider her behavior unusual.

The Rorschach record was one response repeated 10 times. She started with a plant and changed this to a flower on card II; after I asked if it was a red flower, she subsequently called each card a flower of a different color, whether the card was colored or not. The drawings scored considerably higher than the intelligence test, but the parts of the body were misplaced. The ears were on top of the head; two arms are on one side of the body, and another arm was on the opposite side. She also stated first that one arm was the stomach and another the arm.

M. was free and fluent during the standardized doll play interview. She was encouraged to play with the Krall dollhouse (1953). She introduced many additional figures to the doll play, calling all of them by name. There was considerable fluidity in all her productions. She would begin with one figure, doing something; then, that same person was the one watching or listening to the other figure. For example, "Travis doll, he going to play some piano, he going to play piano, listen to Vanessa playing." So Travis begins to play and then is listening to Vanessa. Again, "I'm going to let Travis listen to music," repeated twice. "He going to play Skip to my Lou, and then Travis going to sing ABCs, he going to sing some ABCs watch Dr. K. . . ." Again, the object becomes the subject. Subsequent play has the children going to bed, wrapping Vanessa up in Kleenex, which she called a brown blanket, and some discussion of the crib not belonging in the bathroom. Then she said, "she went to the hisses when she shocks" (and that is as close as could be understood). She went on to play that they were bunk beds and explored the chest of drawers; then she had the children watching Creature Features on TV. Then there was the following sequence: "Vanessa going to stay the night at Travis' house, she going to stay the night at Aunt Emma's house. Where's Keith, that's a girl, that's cousin Ellen, that's not Keith." This suggested additional difficulty differentiating the sex of dolls. She played some more with the dolls at the piano, meanwhile getting many more dolls, and becoming concerned with prohibitions. "Anyone can make the noise at the piano, Vanessa is not going to make no noise at the piano, I want anyone to sit down, Keith better sit down."

There was some more play with furniture, and she began to move things from another dollhouse to the one that she was playing with. "This is Vanessa right here, Markey's things are coming. Come on, get in, kick the door (She moved the door from one house to the other). This one sleeps on the. . . . She can't kick on the door, Charlie Brown never stand up." At this point, she asked to go to the washroom, and she spent some time there. When she returned, her play concerned putting pampers on the baby doll. "Baby Vanessa again, where'd that other baby Vanessa go. She has pretty diapers, plenty of diapers, Pampers, somebody can't keep the baby drier, this is baby Shelley, what's this? (That's baby Shelley.)" She laughed and said, "you baby, baby Shelley, baby Vanessa." Here she seemed to be having some difficulty that there were two baby dolls, and she seemed concerned that she was calling both Vanessa. She needed some help to differentiate that there were two dolls; one could be called Vanessa and one could be called Shelley. Thus, one figure could easily become another and her object differentiations were not stable.

The presence of language and a fantasy life placed this child beyond the autistic phase of development. Also, the child's early infancy as described is not typically autistic. The instability of object representations and inappropriateness of her communications suggested a psychosis. The precipitating factor in her disturbance might have been the 10-day hospitalization at 8 months of age. However, her mother was symbiotically tied to this child (continuing to dress her even at the time of referral), and there seemed to be a lack of differentiation between mother and child. The autistic features seen in the school and at the time of initial referral (i.e., lack of eye contact and lack of relatedness) seemed to be a secondary autism.

This child was in treatment with me for about 11 years, at the end of which time she was transferred to the Adolescent Clinic for medication follow-up, and later seen in the Adult Clinic for follow-up and medication. She was seen initially twice a week in treatment. Her early sessions revealed the level of regression. In her first session, she calmly walked over to the highchair, sat in it, fed the baby doll, and talked about her diapers being dry and that she didn't need to have her diapers washed. It emerged that that was because she (baby) was wearing Pampers. However, inappropriate verbalizations also intruded, such as "lettuce, cabbage, Pampers." Starting with this session, I began to use some of the intrusive therapy techniques when this type of fragmentation occurred. I had her point to her eyes, nose, my eyes,nose, and so forth; count my fingers; and tell me the color of her eyes and hair and my eyes. This seemed to reintegrate her. During this first session and at the end of it, she talked of a child being injured or killed and worried that she would not be coming back. She was reassured that she would be seen twice a week.

An early theme was how many candies she would be given. This provided a conflict, as her mother wanted the amount of candy limited. She imitated the conflict by telling me repeatedly that I should eat everything on my plate. This was mother's admonition to her. Her play moved from the doll play, as she had done in the diagnostic session, and naming the various dolls and feeding them, to interest in objects in the room. She quickly began to take over her own structuring. She named pictures in a South African calendar; she asked for the colors of things, and she began to ask me to spell things for her. She moved to playing such simple board games as Candyland, and a simple card game of War, which I taught her. She stole the baby bottle to take home and said that the baby would now have to eat baby food, since there was no more bottle in the playroom. She did not immediately give up the highchair and said a fat baby was eating a toy; she laughed when I said a fat M. was eating candy in the highchair.

An example of this move toward reintegration within one session occurred 1 month into the treatment. She asked to paint with fingerpaints. She had to be instructed to use a different stick for each color. Her drawing was a crude dab and stretch of paint of each color. As she worked, she began talking in a very regressed and disjointed way about food. (In the occupational therapist's evaluation, she called each form of the form board a different candy bar name.) I focused on her favorite food, macaroni and cheese. Then I showed her how you can make designs in the paint. She responded, "And get your hands dirty?" I said this was alright. She tentatively made a circle, square, rectangle, and diamond and then asked me to draw a fish, a dolphin, and an elephant. Interestingly, her preoccupation with one of the names of fish was almost identical to her mother's maiden name. Then she went on to have me draw various people she knew. She elicited each part of the figure: Now draw her eyes, her nose, her mouth, her ears, her hair. With these activities, she reintegrated up the developmental scale, from a purely oral regression, to interest in symbols and animals, and to people, becoming well integrated and structured by the end of this activity. As we finished, she helped in washing and cleaning up. She then went to her favorite place, to look at the lake. The ritual here was to repeat that fish and a dolphin lived in the lake. She spelled a name on a truck and asked me to spell the names of children she knew at school.

M. began to demonstrate a need to control the therapist in these games, and her behavior at home became more impulsive as well as controlling. She was punished for throwing peanut shells out the window and for picking up a baby, for fear that she might drop it. Her subsequent play sessions revolved around these two events. She played being the baby, who would fall off the table. She needed reassurance that the therapist would not let her be hurt but that she was too heavy to catch in this way. Finally, in later sessions, she began to act these concerns out in more symbolic ways with the dolls. Dolls were picked up and held and then dropped. She said in one session that they were going to get squirrel nuts: Did white babies mess with nuts, and what did their mothers do? Did white mothers let white babies mess with nuts? I said, "yes," and I asked whether black babies messed with nuts what happened. She said, "They get a whupping with an iron cord, or whip, or belt." I asked if that hurt. First she said yes, then no. It seemed a new stage of development that the working through of these traumatic events was being done in symbolic play at a higher level than the body language of falling off the chair or table.

Table 6-1. Cognitive Growth during Treatment[a]

C.A.	M.A.	VIQ	PIQ	FIQ	Drawing standard scores
6–7	3–10	54	(Binet)		77
7–9	4–5	55	(Binet)		74 (girl); 69 (boy)
	WPPSY	70	67	69	
9–0	5–4	57	(Binet)		
9–8	WISC-R	64	70	64	79 (girl); 77 (boy)
10–11	WISC-R	81	99	88	
14–1	WISC-R	72	84	76	48 (girl); 59 (boy)

[a]C.A., chronological age; M.A., mental age; VIQ, verbal intelligence quotient; PIQ, performance intelligence quotient; FIQ, full intelligence quotient.

These developmental shifts could be traced in the psychological test examinations that were administered during the course of treatment. They can be seen most dramatically in the shift of IQ. (See Table 6-1.)

The first and fourth testings were done by myself; the second, third and last testings were done by students; and the 10–11 testing was done by the staff psychologist at her school. We can note that her best functioning was with myself and with the experienced examiner at her school. She showed really poor functioning on the early Binet tests and did best on the Wechsler type tests. It is hard to explain the really poor scores on the latest figure drawings. It is probable that they were invalid either because of difference in scoring norms or perhaps because of the upset of being tested by an unfamiliar examiner.

It was believed by myself and later examiners that her highest level of ego functioning was that of a borderline personality disorder. These shifts in cognitive functioning from familiar to unfamiliar examiners may reflect the fluidity of her ego state and the lack of cohesiveness of ego when stressed. The dénouement in the therapy was the dramatic revelation of her fear of the gun that associated to the magazine picture of the man with blood streaming from his eyes.

At about this time in the treatment, she revealed the vertical split in her personality organization, or ego structure. She looked in the one-way vision mirror in the room in which we were meeting and stated, "That is Gethesme, and I am M." When asked who Gethesme might be, she answered, "that is the bad me." We can see the relationship in the treatment between the early echolalic preoccupations with prohibitions and punishments and this vertical split. The treatment was then able to evolve into help with her sensitivity to criticism and what she perceived as slights, hurts, and punishments.

The follow-up supportive care at our clinic aided this now young adult to move away from our city to a small city, where she and mother live with her older brother and his wife and two children. She recently wrote to me, telling me that she is studying for her GED, and "I am really trying."

7

THE BORDERLINE CHILD

Treatment of the borderline child has many similarities to the treatment of more severely disturbed psychotic children. These children also often have little access to secondary process thinking and show an incapacity to reflect on conflicts and dynamic issues and/or to verbalize these. Even older borderline children may have to be approached by nonverbal modes. An effective mode of treatment for them is play action. They may claim that they are too old to play, but they are sometimes almost totally inaccessible in a verbal mode. As treatment progresses, play action may be more largely given up and replaced with verbal therapy.

The older borderline child may be fixated at a developmental level that is preverbal, and impulse and action oriented. Ekstein (1966) described a developmental sequence from acting out of unconscious conflict, to play action, to fantasy, to secondary process thought. Before secondary process modes have developed and there is delay of action, acting-out modes prevail. The next step in the developmental sequence is play action. Play is the communicative free-associative process of childhood.

To develop and be present, it presupposes a certain maturation of the ego. Ekstein described play action as a "complex mental phenomenon which includes the act, the phantasy, advanced elements of language and frequently strong aspects of reality testing" (1966, p. 171). He differentiated between "acting out as experimental recollection; of play action as the slow replacement of impulsive and inappropriate action by a more advanced form of thinking; of play acting as an initial identification with a fantasied object in order to master the future experimentally; and of fantasy as a higher form of play action in which the need for action is given up" (1966, p. 171).

Play action may represent different levels of conscious and unconscious control and can represent communications of different levels of development and awareness. If used in the treatment of the preadolescent or adolescent patient, it is possible to understand and correct by means of the communicated play action, the underlying unconscious conflicts expressed by the play. One can then strengthen the ego structures so that phantasy is replaced by secondary process understanding and expression of the conflict. This may involve communications and interpretations at the differing levels communicated. At the point that the patient is beginning to express more material at a conscious level and with secondary process communication, he may be able to begin to express the conflict in verbal terms, and the play action may be given up as the exclusive form of treatment.

Case Example: G. The play-action mode of treatment was selected for our 11-year-old male patient G. because he presented himself as having no problems and he answered all verbal questions with the statement: "That's personal." G. was the oldest of two children in an intact family. The younger sister was a handicapped child with cerebral palsy, to whom both parents were devoted. It was recommended that G. be evaluated at the time his sister was being evaluated because he was doing poorly in school and not performing to capacity. His problem began when he entered kindergarten; his parents also reported that he had never gotten along with peers. He had been seen in a previous community and was described as being "full of anxieties" by the previous examiners. The parents described G. as being a sensitive child who worried about people. When John F. Kennedy was assassinated, he built a wooden casket and draped a flag over it. When the funeral was over, he commented: "They've buried him at last." His mother described his keeping this casket and his talking about Oswald every night and attempting to get his mother to say that she hated Oswald. G. was happy when Ruby killed Oswald. When his mother explained that it's never good to kill, G. questioned her as to why policemen wore guns. His mother also reported confusion regarding religion. G. asked questions such as why God allowed President Kennedy to be killed.

His mother described G. as reacting to ridicule by teachers and peers, particularly regarding his poor penmanship, by coming home in tears, throwing his books in the incinerator, and retreating further into his shell. His mother identified with his sensitivity and saw G. as having something to contribute to the world. She emphasized his profound thinking on problems far beyond his years ("Where did the first seed come from?" and "Who said there are 24 hours in a day?") yet his inability to learn fundamentals. The father's assessment of G. was similar to that of the mother. He saw him as "sensitive" and thought that the child might have a career later in life in religion or social work. He did comment that the emphasis on religion in the parochial school he was attending might not be good for him, as he "thinks too deeply" and is preoccupied with the crucifixion and Christ being nailed to the cross. He described him as always relating better to adults than to peers and as often being the butt of teasing and ridicule by peers. G. was described as having poor physical coordination; repeated testing both before and during treatment indicated a lower nonverbal than verbal measure on the intelligence tests.

Initially, G. denied having any problems, except that hangings bothered him, like on the TV program "Bonanza." His perception of coming to the clinic was: "I thought I was coming here to paint." I was reminded of his experience at the parochial school, where they did not force him to do schoolwork but let him paint instead. Early sessions were spent painting and playing out scenes with the Krall dollhouse. His paintings were of trolls, and he brought in his own puppets. In his first dollhouse scene, he pictured two scenes in which children did things about which the parents were angry and for which the children were punished. This play took place in a setting of many demands to me, for candy and paper, and required the setting of many limits. Another frequent play during the early sessions during the first year of treatment was his tendency to cover up his thoughts and feelings by saying that these were personal and he was not going to tell me. He took charge of my credenza and made it his own property, of which he was the boss during the session.

G. was preoccupied with hair and in particular had a preoccupation with the Rapunzel fairy tale. This seemed to serve two dynamic needs. One seemed to have to do with power, or the counterphobic aspect of castration anxiety. The other, perhaps not essentially different, was the masculine–feminine dimension. G. told me that he wanted to become a hairdresser. It was interesting to note that while many things were personal, G. was quite free in presenting this material. His concern about the story of Rapunzel was that the child was given away, but he said that it was better for the people to give the child to the witch than to let the mother die. During this time, he was oppositional and he seemed to be concerned over good and bad behavior. He continued to test me as to what he could and could not do. He painted a picture of a lonely flower that didn't have any friends to visit, and he wrote a story about this. He complained of his jealousy of a cousin who would always leave him to play with friends.

G. put me in positions in which he could be in control. He made me a dunce cap and his mother a crown. At the same time, he was having serious reality problems, which he began to talk about in treatment. He talked about the man who had exposed himself to him in the park toilet when he was at day camp, and he spoke about similar problems with boys in the school toilet. He began having difficulty with boys who ganged up on him in school. He was so frightened that often he would remain home after lunch because of his fear of returning to school, as the boys threatened to harm him on the way home. He would remain in the classroom until the other children had left, for the same reason. We talked about this and did some practice fighting. I encouraged him to stand up for himself. As he was often very provocative and threatening to me, leaning over me and hitting me, I called attention to this fighting behavior with me as a contradiction to his fear of fighting the boys. During this period, he requested repeatedly that I spank him.

Very early, G. set up a role-reversal situation in which he was the teacher and I the pupil. He then gave me work to do, and he became the bossy teacher who told me what to do and corrected my work. This activity took a large part of the year and much of the time was spent in the auditorium, where G. could use the blackboard. Gradually, G. began to ask me to be the teacher. Sometimes he would do the work assigned, and sometimes he played the bad boy whom I had to reprimand, just as he had told me I was bad and had to sit in the corner. Some doll play was concerned with children who ran away or were bad and got punished. The doll play then shifted to sexual and religious preoccupations. He would marry two doll figures, or in play action he would marry me and then kiss me. He also played out his confirmation and acted as the priest, who would then slap me on the cheek. The play movement appeared to be from provocative, controlling, hostile behavior, to playing out the affectionate, close feelings. Even these, however, were accompanied by some need to direct aggression toward me, as in the religious confirmation ceremony.

There was a 2-month break in the treatment when the patient was at camp and the therapist on vacation. On return, he appeared to be less provocative, and he was able to share that he was having some "sickening thoughts," that bothered him. This represented the first indication of something internal of which he was aware, that was not directed in action play or behavior.

He was preoccupied with such things as sucking another boy's penis and putting one's face in someone's bottom. He felt it was wrong to have such thoughts. The therapist suggested that this was a normal part of growing up, to be curious about one's body. He said that when he was 5 years old he and another boy showed each other their penises. I thought they were just experimenting. G. continued to bring up these thoughts and also made some tentative attempts to act them out. He reported that he put his bottom in his sister's bottom, and he was told that this was wrong because she could not protect herself.

G. became preoccupied with sexual things that stimulated him in treatment, for instance, catching a glimpse of the therapist's underclothes when he leaned over to pick up a checker. Gradually, he revealed distortion about marriage. He thought that you kissed someone's bottom after marrying and that two men could marry one another. However, he also later indicated a rather complete knowledge of reproduction.

He also played out some scenes of me being the maid who was fired and of married people who visit and get killed; he then spent many sessions marrying a couple, initially two men. Many times he wanted to have me, as the preacher, marry them in the bathroom. The final time he played this out, he wanted to jump on the table for the honeymoon.

There was a sequence of dramatic play around Halloween when he brought in a wig, and he played out over and over again that a thief poses as a butler or maid, is dewigged, and found out, when they steal the boss's jewels and valuables. He dressed up in smock and wig, and he seemed to enjoy the dressing up. I handled some of this material by diverting the discussion into what his trolls would wear for Halloween and what he and his friends would wear.

G. began to act out his positive and sexual feelings for me by jumping into my lap and kissing me and pushing himself hard into my lap, and then falling into the floor as if in a faint. I set a limit on all touching, including hitting and kissing, pointing out that he was 13 years old and too big a boy for this behavior. This became an issue in subsequent sessions. G. asked frequently why he couldn't touch me, since he used to be able to do this; the limit had to be repeated frequently. He understood that getting too close was too "sexy," as he described it; he gradually accepted the fact that he was a teenager and that this behavior was inappropriate, although he continued to test me.

Gradually, he began not to reveal his thoughts anymore; instead, he would call me on the telephone to ask me whether it would be alright to wrap something around his penis or put something up his rectum, and whether it would be wrong to rape one's sister. About this time, he undressed in front of his friend and his friend's 20-year-old cousin; he said he was experimenting. I told him the behavior was wrong and that he could get into trouble and be hurt by such behavior and that mother took a dim view of such experimentation.

He was giving me incredible amounts of schoolwork at this time. He buried himself in his homework and would make these phone calls to tell me his disturbing thoughts. I called to his attention that he was not talking to me in my office but making these distressing calls. I said that he could no longer call me except to say hello, that I could not deal with his problems on the phone, and that he would have to talk in the office. He became angry with me. First, he said people were listening in the hall, and the phone call was private—he trusted his parents and me. When it was pointed out that no one was listening, he said he was embarrassed. As a defense, he resisted my efforts to get him to give up the schoolwork. Finally, we arrived at a compromise: we would play school as long as it did not interfere with his talking to me, and he could call me to say hello. The movement during this phase of treatment was from purely play action to a more verbal mode of interchange with some stereotyped school play continuing.

The next 4 months of treatment was a transitional phase from play action to more active verbal sessions. In the early part of this phase, the play action involved a murder game in which I was a murderer brought to trial. I was to admit my guilt or demonstrate that I had an alibi. There would be neither lawyers or jurors, and I would be sentenced to the electric chair. G. strapped me into the electric chair, and G. would get fairly excited and would invariably hit me in the breast. He was also discussing his preoccupation with which form of death I would choose: hanging, decapitation, being burned at the stake, or electrocution. He was preoccupied with Joan of Arc's having been burned at the stake and with whether she was alive at the time.

Being tied to a chair as well as his excitement in these episodes became somewhat frightening to me. I told G. that we could no longer play, and we would spend the session talking. He said that he had hoped for some time that I would make him talk. Nevertheless, a primarily verbal approach was quite difficult. The nature of the interchange during the verbal sessions assumed the proportions of a pitched battle, in which G. tested out who was to be in control. His frequent question was "who said?" He then objected if you didn't respond, "I said," but if you do, he asked, "Is it that way because you said it." The controlling form of the play action entered the verbal situation. He tried to resist talking and to establish that I was saying that I was the boss. Eventually, I did this. I told G. that I wanted to sit in my seat and that this was my office—that I was the doctor and the boss in here. Finally, at the end of these sessions, he would admit to having something bothering him.

For example, he had a dream in which he was sucking someone's penis, but he decided that the way to handle these fears was to act them out. I said that thoughts and dreams could not hurt him but that it was wrong to act on them. There were other instances of sexual concern and curiosity. Could boys have babies? Was it wrong to let your penis stick out of your clothes in your own room? There were two kinds of episodes of acting out during this period. G. engaged in an exposure of his penis with his friends' cousin and rubbed his leg for a quarter. He also told of burning a puppet at the stake with his friend. I took the position with both episodes that it was wrong to do these things. G. began to prepare again to go to camp and expressed fears that the boys would again make fun of him and call him names, and he was afraid of being homesick. He had made some progress in dealing with his problems at a more secondary process level in the verbal mode.

G. wrote from camp to tell me that he still had problems, and he wanted to continue to see me, as he thought we could work them out. He was concerned about the separation and about losing me again; he expressed some of this concern by worrying about people putting babies up for adoption. His sexual concerns came up in the form of being preoccupied with sexual thoughts that he would not talk about during the interview. He wanted to call me at home about these thoughts. He was concerned what I might write in his notes that his mother might see. The content of these thoughts was related to his sexual play with a boy at the church.

He was re-evaluated after 2½ years of treatment with psychological testing on his return from camp, and the psychologist recommended a male therapist. It was suggested that since transition had been made to verbal therapy, transfer to another therapist could be effected. The advantages of a male model for identification purposes outweighed the disadvantages of interrupting the transference with the female therapist. It was decided that we would try conjoint treatment, once a week with each therapist, for a period of time to ease his separation from me and to help him make the transition (see Krall & Irvin, 1973). G. initially said that he loved the new therapist, but when the time came to see him, his attitude changed. He preferred the psychologist who tested him, and he made efforts to see him. He said he disliked the new therapist and hated him, and then the examiner as well. When I told him that he should rather be angry at me because I carried out the recommendation, he found this difficult. He became concerned with whether I would fire the tester or the new therapist, and I was able to relate this to his concern as to whether I would fire him as a patient. He talked about the suddenness of the transfer. Gradually, material began to emerge that had the feeling of reminiscence about all the things we had done together since we started treatment. He wanted to look at his notes or to have old objects replaced (GI Joe) to recapture the past memories. He began treatment with the new male therapist, and a sign of growth was his ability to come by himself by bus. This was not without much ambivalence on his parents' part, and with some fear on his part. But he also enjoyed the freedom and reported that it was either fun or boring.

G. began to be concerned about Christ and the crucifixion during this series of sessions. At one point, I commented on some sores he had on his hands. He said that he had done it with nails—no, with a pen. I commented that I was concerned that he was hurting himself and that he was not Christ. He said that I was making fun of him. I said I was not making fun of him, that I didn't want him to hurt himself, and that he did not have to prove that he rose in order to prove that Christ rose from the dead. He tested out my concern many times: Would I stop him from doing such and such, from picking a scab, and so forth? Many times, G. wanted me to paint either Christ being crucified or Joan at the stake. I would refuse to do this but would not prevent his drawing these things. I hoped that someday he wouldn't have to do this. One day he said he was not going to do it any more, and he threw the drawings into the wastebasket.

G. was going through an oppositional struggle with the male therapist. He tested out his relationship with him by leaving sessions early. He would contact me just before his session with him. Later he made attempts to see him before he saw me or after he saw me. He would go by his office in order to do so, even if it was to whisper, "I hate you," at the door. The male therapist and I met with him to tell him that if he was to come to the clinic he would have to see both of us and would have to keep to the rules. There would be no loitering outside the offices; he would wait in the waiting room and leave by the clinic.

G. worked through some feelings of rivalry with another patient, by wanting material just like hers with which to make puppets. He had for a long time wanted something she had given me, a sand dollar, which was like one I had given him when I returned from vacation. His sibling rivalry feelings had their biggest test when his sister was hospitalized. Initially, he could not talk of his fears for her, but when she returned home he was able to say that he was scared she would die and that he had lost his faith in doctors.

He began to become concerned with fire. He was finally able to say that the reason he was preoccupied with fire was not that he was scared of it or interested in it, as I had suggested, but that it could hurt people.

After the joint meeting with both therapists, sessions became more controlling. He would ask me whether I loved him and then became extremely bossy and demanding. He wanted to be able to contact me at home as a friend. He was angry when I pointed out that I could not be his social friend, that he was my patient, and that my time at home was mine in which to rest.

There was a continuation of the sexual preoccupations. He confronted me with what I would do if he took his penis out in my office. I related this to his having put his penis in his sister's hands at home. He found a female friend in the waiting room and became very attached to her. To me he was bossy, demanding, and insulting, but he also wanted to get very close to me. He became interested in male models who have little clothes on; he brought pictures of them. He said he wanted to leave treatment, but in the same breath he would ask to call and to visit me at home. He became very angry when limits were set. He seemed to be dealing with transference issues: closeness and distance, a female patient friend, and interest in male models. He asked to paint alongside me, then painted over my painting and destroyed it. He became angry when I told him he did this because he was jealous; he sent a note with his mother that he didn't know what he would do if I ever said that again. In that same session, he dumped over the ashtray and asked if I would clean it up. When I said yes, and started to clean it up, he cleaned it and said he was showing me he could be more responsible. The preoccupation with Christ and Joan of Arc gave way to preoccupation with fire. He wanted to build me a record player that also had a fireplace in it.

The next phase of treatment began with his asking to bring in his record player, which he promised to play very quietly. There was a perseverative preoccupation with the Brandenburg Fifth concerto, of which there was only a small sample on a record of Great Masters that he had been given some years before. As he began this phase of treatment, he revisited some early themes, as if to recapitulate the treatment process. He played with the dollhouse, reminiscent of sessions of previous years. The difference was that the wedding partners names were eventually that of the male therapist. He also played out the birth scene.

The remaining series of sessions to the termination phase involved music. He reminded me of an earlier promise that the clinic would buy the Brandenburg Fifth for Christmas for him. In the earliest sessions, he was controlling. He wanted me to pretend to be playing the violin and he would conduct. As time went on, however, he evidenced considerable interest in composers. He composed a song about Joan of Arc. He also became interested in the Oz stories. He was preoccupied with whether the straw man and the wooden man would burn if caught in a fire. He tried to pin the blame for a broken hinge on my phonograph onto the male therapist. I told him at this time that he had my permission to like him. He said he didn't want to take it: "He's too personal, he's a busy body." During periods of upset when he blamed him for destructiveness to the records, some mention of Christ as the prophet re-emerged. He informed me that he was going to write some compositions and send them to me on vacation. His story concerned the Pumpkin being burned in a fire and turning into a tart.

On return from vacation, I presented him with some Beethoven concertos. I had also earlier given him my duplicate third and fourth Brandenburg Concertos. He was pleased with this gift, but very demanding when there was no plastic cover for them. He claimed he was nervous because the kids were acting up at school. He went on to tell me that he could not talk to his father, who wouldn't talk about Joan of Arc or Bach, and only wants to talk about places where women take off their clothing. Is there a place where men take off their clothing? At the same time, he gave me a small monkey and said: "See no evil, hear no evil, speak no evil."

G. began to struggle with his feelings about termination. He began to ask me about myself and how much longer he would be coming in to see me. I informed him I would be tapering off seeing him after Christmas (in September). Where or when would he see me again? He became more clinging, showed me his sores frequently, asking me if they were infected and were healing. He came to sessions very early. He wrote many more stories and asked to get them typed by the psychology secretary. He talked of buying the camp he used to go to, as it was going out of business. He would let me stay there for a free vacation, but the male therapist would have to pay. When I said that he would let him go to the resort, he was very quiet.

Previous symptoms briefly re-emerged. He was involved in some sex play with a male peer, and he lit candles at home. He began to give me many going-away gifts, starting with a goldfish that he gave early because it might die. He was concerned that his mother said his sister would die. He told me that we had had our disagreements but that we had gotten over them. He became concerned about an article that said that colored TVs blow up. I said that I had read the same article and that it also said it wouldn't happen if you pulled the plug, and I had pulled the plug. He was concerned whether the Tin Man was alive. How could he still be alive?

Throughout all these sessions, the general pattern was to play and record various Beethoven and Bach pieces on the tape recorder, with conversation ensuing over the music. The shift from oppositional, demanding, and manipulative behavior to that of cooperation was dramatic after we had introduced the music into the sessions. G. gradually moved from an exclusive interest in the Brandenburg Fifth to many other pieces of music. He checked records out of the library and joined a record club.

At this time, our plan was that the male therapist would terminate with G. in March. G. was continuing to say that he only liked Dr. I. that much—a little. He denied that he went to see him because he liked him. He said that he didn't like him because he got too close to him. He sat in this chair, and then he moved away. I reminded that he used to not like my sitting too close to him. He said, "You didn't like to sit too close to me." I said, "I didn't because it used to upset you." I ascribed his present upset condition to his knowing that we would no longer be supporting him. At this time, G. asked to see Dr. I. for 1 more year. He could only say vaguely that he didn't benefit from only seeing him 1 year. I reminded him of his fear of closeness and tendency to tell him that things were personal. He agreed that he could attempt to overcome this problem with him. Upon agreement, it was decided that G. would see Dr. I for 6 months and that if he continued to use the treatment, this would be extended to 1 year.

Sessions with me continued to be concerned with termination. G. reminisced about earlier times together and began to bring me gifts—pink roses from church and a candy dish he made in home mechanics class. He dealt with the relationship between me and Dr. I. He was concerned about his sister and about whether there would ever be a cure for her illness. He gave me more gifts, a small leather puppy and a small pencil set. I asked him what all the gifts meant. He said, "So you will not forget me." I told him that I would not forget him and that I did not need all the gifts to remind me of him. During this termination phase of treatment, modeling and introjective type of behavior went on. He wanted to know what my opinions were about music. He found it nice that now we both had the Brandenburg Fifth. He said he gave me the puppy because he had three of them, just as I gave him the Brandenburg Third and Fourth because I had two of these. He tried to set up the future, that he would be allowed to write to me.

Could he see me after another child's session? Before her session? Could he telephone me? Could he buy records from the C.R. club, as I did? If he got a college education, could he work here? Would I watch the same TV show as he? The separation and termination themes were interwoven with his wanting us to be just alike, his attempts at introjection, or in self-psychology terms, twinning. When I commented on this to G. and wondered whether he remembered his wanting to be doing the same thing as me, he said that he used to be demanding. G. ended his sessions by asking me whether it was alright to love one's doctor. I said, "of course." He said his mother loved me and that he loved me. He had asked whether I loved him and whether he was my favorite patient. I answered, "one of my favorites." I said I had a very special kind of love for him. He had earlier asked me whether he could kiss me goodbye, and when I said no, he said, "Well, a very good firm handshake would do as well."

Subsequent to these sessions, G. continued to maintain some contact before and after his sessions with Dr. I. and through telephone calls, which I limited to one a week. He continued contact with Dr. I. with phone calls after he terminated with him. After some time away from the clinic, he initiated clinic contact for some help with career planning as a young adult. He lingered to say hello to me for awhile during this recontact of the clinic but gave this behavior up after some discussion with his new therapist.

The 5-year treatment period developed from play action in the controlling and demanding transference to evidence of this in his later verbal treatment. He demonstrated splits in his view of objects, mother, and therapist and in his view of himself as the bad object that had to be punished. There were primitive concerns with objects who had been severely punished, Christ and Joan of Arc. The preoccupation with fire seemed to relate to this but also to his fear of annihilation and dissolution. He was concerned with abandonment and had early concerns that if he transferred affection to the therapist the mother would die or disappear. He expressed concerns about babies put up for adoption and more direct fears that he would lose the therapist and the therapy. The sexual preoccupations were first expressed in the play action during marriage ceremonies and only later in the verbal therapy. The play-action phase of treatment permitted direct access to the fantasy and enabled the patient to express his concerns without having to face them directly through secondary process thought. He viewed his inner thoughts and personal fantasy as too personal to express directly in words. Even though he later expressed so eloquently "I have been hoping you would make me talk," he fought exploring his inner life in more secondary process terms with obstinacy and controllingness.

8

NARCISSISTIC PERSONALITY DISORDERS

Narcissistic personality disorders show a wide variety of symptom pictures and of character development, ranging from those with limited and impoverished intellectual and creative capacities to those with higher levels of intellectual ability. The derivation of the disorder is within a similar phase of development to borderline cases, beginning at 2–3 years of age or slightly earlier, during the later phases of separation and individuation, as described by Mahler (1967). The major differentiation between the borderline conditions and the narcissistic conditions was defined by Kohut (1983) as a cohesive sense of self.

Kohut defines a separate line of development for narcissism, from autoeroticism to narcissism to higher transformations of narcissism. He differentiated this line of development from that going from autoeroticism via narcissism to object love. He divides the narcissistic line of development into two principal branches: the grandiose self, and the idealized parental imago. He believes that, unlike borderline cases and the psychoses, those fixated or regressed to archaic narcissistic levels of development could form a narcissistic transference, with the analyst as self-object. Kohut differentiates between object relations and object love:

> The antithesis to narcissism is not the object relation but object love. An individual's profusion of object relations, in the sense of the observer of the social field, may conceal his narcissistic experience of the object world; and a person's seeming isolation and loneliness may be the setting for a wealth of current object investments. (1983, p. 228)

In the transference neurosis, there is a re-enactment of earlier object and libido conflicts through the transference neurosis. The narcissistic transference is used to interpret directly the re-enactment of the grandiose self in the mirroring transference and of the idealized parental imago in the idealizing transference. Kohut later added the twinning transference and that of merger for some patients.

In my psychotherapy work with children with narcissistic problems, I have found that some of these features are very much in evidence. The principles suggested by this line of thought can be helpful in working with children who have developed grandiose and omnipotent defenses against underlying feelings of helplessness and vulnerability. They seem to be enmeshed in these struggles in spite of indications that, for some, later development has occurred. Neurotic symptoms and issues may occur side by side with these more primitive concerns. Because the origin of narcissistic aspects of the personality is so early, these aspects are often preverbal. Thus, access to these materials with children may often be best addressed through play, fantasy, and play action.

Case Example: J. The case discussed in this chapter demonstrates the use of play and play-action techniques with children with narcissistic disorders. The child was a 9-year-old boy, when I initially saw him. He had been seen by a psychiatrist for 8 months and was discharged because his initial symptoms had remitted and he seemed to be at a plateau in treatment. I saw him 4 months later. His parents brought him back for treatment at our clinic because he had reacted so drastically to the termination. He screamed that he felt like he had lost his best friend and said that he was sorry that he had not told his therapist what was bothering him, playing games instead of his telling him what was wrong.

His initial referral symptoms to our clinic were his phobic response to darkness, not sleeping in his own bed, and his fears of being poisoned by his mother. His mother also described him as sleeping "stiffly" and of never being able to relax, as being easily frustrated and nervous, and of eating and immediately defecating afterward. His symptoms were dated to the death of a maternal great grandfather who died of cancer in the home after a 3-month illness. J. saw him during the wake and wanted to touch him; he described him as looking as though he were sleeping. In school at that time, he was reported to have been frightened by an allegedly sadistic and hypochondriacal teacher who discussed diseases at length. He was also reported to be absent from school for 2 weeks. When the school sent a truant officer and nurse to the house, they found that he had a low-grade temperature of 99.4°F and itching and rash of the rectum. Additional difficulties reported by the parents were that he began to steal after school ended: "He didn't know what to do with himself." He would have money, and they did not know where it came from. He also became afraid of going into the front room, and he had to have his younger brother in with him, until he began to be afraid. He began to refuse to take a bath and had a fear of drowning in the bathtub. His mother had to undress him and drop him into the bathtub. Afraid of sleeping in his top bunk bed, he had been sleeping on the living room couch. He was very nervous and would sit on the toilet and bring in 15 books to calm himself down. He would sit there for a while and say that his stomach felt really bad. He would read a few pages to his father; then he would say that he felt better and would lie on the couch. His parents described his pressure of speech as making them nervous. He would get wound up and become increasingly nervous; they would react by becoming nervous themselves. He was also constantly fighting with his younger brother. J. and his mother would scream at each other. He was described as asking questions he knew the answer to, as beating his brother or mother, and as doing things to aggravate his mother. He watched TV or read for hours but was otherwise tearing up the house or being aggravating. On the positive side, he would go to his grandmother's for several hours, and on return would behave wonderfully.

The child's father attributed the illness to the older women of the family sitting around the table in J.'s presence and talking of death and illness. His mother attributed its onset to the death of her grandfather and that of her aunt: "She was like a grandma to him." Six months after her death, J. would ask whether Nana had died because he lied and whether Jana (grandfather) had also died because he told lies. He would talk night after night as to whether they had died because of his lies.

The patient lived with his father, mother, and 3-years-younger brother. He was born prematurely, and his mother was vague about his developmental milestones. She had had a postpartum depression at the birth of his younger brother, during which time her mother and sister cared for J. (he was about 3 years of age). No other separations were reported, and he had never been hospitalized. He had two accidents: one at age 2, hitting his head on the TV, and when he was hit in the head during the current year with a bat. His reaction to the latter event was that he was going to die but would first tell his relatives that he loved them. "Why did this happen to me? I'm disfigured." Nobody would love him. His only childhood disease was chicken pox.

The diagnostic evaluation at this time included psychological testing. J. was found to be of superior intelligence. J. had initially presented as a phobic neurotic boy who was displaying obsessional defenses following his great grandfather's death, mother's postpartum depression after the birth of his brother, and his father's increased unavailability. The plan of treatment at that time was to have him work through the maternal grandfather's death and the fears of retaliation touched off by this event. Initially, he was anxious and running around, pretending he was an airplane. Then the anxiety level subsided, and he would have grandiose flying fantasies and feel strong and powerful. The therapy was largely nonverbal. Considerable time was spent at the blackboard, drawing pictures of monsters and ghosts eating each other up. He demonstrated a preoccupation with Va Voom, which encapsulated everything, swallowed everything, and eventually destroyed himself. There was work with separation anxiety and peekaboo. As time went on, this obsession modulated and became less intense, and he could draw on paper. He began to act out his anxiety in gestures and to use words. He began to collect things, and his games become obsessional. He played war games with soldiers; this phase lasted many months. As treatment became stalemated and he was showing improvement at home and school, termination was planned and completed. The psychiatrist believed that the basic core of separation anxiety and the death were never dealt with. He agreed that a further course of treatment might be necessary to deal with these issues.

The new diagnostic material, from testing and two diagnostic interviews with J., suggested that there had been development in the form of greater obsessional control of the anxiety and somatic symptoms. These problems had returned with termination from the first treatment. The question raised at this time was whether the return to anxiety represented an abandonment in the sense of a separation from a figure with whom he had symbiotically fused. Was it a re-enactment of his feared separation from the symbiotic mother or of his real separation from this symbiotic fusion when his younger brother was born and mother was less available to him? Or was he locked in a narcissistic union with his psychiatrist, who represented a secondary ego to him, through which he had been able to modulate the anxiety?

The current diagnostic material suggested that underlying the severe phobic and somatic preoccupations and the obsessive defenses, there was a strong narcissistic core. The earlier treatment suggested a preoccupation with grandiose and omnipotent power. One could speculate that the loss of grandfather and great aunt stirred up in him not only the loss and separations, but the fear that his own grandiosity destroyed them. Did they die because I lied to them? He believed that, with the separation from his doctor, he would die. Yet he very easily made contact with me and was "happy" for me to be his therapist. He was narcissistically injured when I suggested that he should think through whether he now wanted a lady doctor. The interviews with him were obsessive and dealt with the phobic and somatic problems, but his test material focused on the neediness and constant searching for oral supplies by a boy who found it difficult to make close relationships. I did not feel that in my early contacts with him it mattered greatly whom he would be in the room with; indeed, after the second diagnostic interview, he said goodbye to the tape recorder.

Genetically, J. had not had his anxieties modulated by either his overprotective mother who clung to him or his more passive unavailable father. The major narcissistic injury may have been the withdrawal of his mother during her depression and the birth of his younger brother simultaneously. A treatment plan would have to be focused on the development of a relationship that would enable him to work through the narcissistic issues that were holding him back from more adequately dealing with his anger, projected anger, and accompanying feelings of being helpless and unprotected.

Complicating these problems were the family's style of focusing on illness and death, although they were willing to attribute this to the teacher in second grade or to other members of their family. Their style led to J.'s feeling continually helpless, unprotected, and vulnerable, focusing on all the bodily feelings associated with illness and possible death. Both parents were in treatment at the time of the referral.

The trends in the treatment of this boy may be identified as follows:

1. Development of idealizing transference with the therapist
2. Deidealization of the previous therapist who terminated him
3. Ability to mourn the loss of the former therapist
4. Clinging to superheroes and grandiosity
5. Gradual increase in interests in "reality" (collecting, giving up exclusive interest in superheroes)
6. Gradual reduction in fears, somatizations, and anxiety; vomiting (fear he would die now disappears)
7. Changes in relationships to brother and to father
    a. Change from extremes of sibling jealousy to a reasonable wish to learn how to get along
    b. Coming to terms with need to idealize father; beginning more realistic appraisal of his relationship with him.
8. Replacement of grandiose and omnipotent fantasy with realistic interests in sports
9. Overt expression of fears of real vulnerabilities (e.g., being hurt in sports, fears of staying over at other people's houses)
10. Termination issues and termination

The early sessions focused on his nervousness and somatic preoccupations and with projection onto the teacher who only talked about illnesses. J. talked of feelings of loss, such as everything he had to leave in his desk at the end of school that his teacher did not let him take. In his initial treatment session, he drew a picture of GI Joe in the tower of gifts found in the bathtub for Christmas, and of the Mad Hatter with eyes that could put anyone to sleep. These drawings seemed to symbolize his need for power and for supplies, as well as his fear of the new relationship. By the third session, he had begun to mirror me and to express some grandiose fantasy, such as having his own TV show. In the fourth session, never having noticed the sink before, he told me as he washed his hands after working with clay figures: "I am the only one in the clinic to have a sink. I am pretty special." He began to identify with powerful figures, such as Evel Knieval. But one of his figures was also the more vulnerable Tin Man. Elvis Presley was also a figure of identification for him: "He is the King. He has been for 20 years. He is a millionaire. He has more money than the president or vice president. He is building an aeroplane with a gymnasium and a flying bathtub." At this time, J.'s mother told me that he was 50% improved. He was now sleeping in his bed but was still deathly afraid of taking a bath. He now began to speak of me as his favorite; he didn't think before that he would want anyone but his previous doctor, and now he said at home that he hoped I would be his doctor forever. This seemed to end the first phase of treatment, the development of an idealizing transference to the therapist, with expressions of the grandiose self.

In the next session, J. talked of a broken window he had mended. The carpenter came to mend the door in my office. He then told me that his mother had really broken the window; he had only gotten the glass, and mother had put the putty in. The spur of the carpenter actually fixing something in my room momentarily broke through his defense of grandiosity. We talked later of his wish to be able to fix things, like father the mechanic, and of his ability to do other things. He could climb a tree and ride a bike on the wheel. This then permitted him to go on with descriptions of the idealized father who bought old cars and fixed them up to sell them. His father had been out of work for a time before this, and it had been difficult to retain his idealization of him. Again, he considered my office special to have a sink, representing the retained idealization of the therapist. He said after a previous session: "This is such a fine office, you could live in it."

Three months into treatment, J. began to engage in grandiose and destructive fantasies with the doll house. Superbaby knocked mother and father down, and male dolls knocked down females, with the men always winning. There was a brief interruption in treatment because of the family's financial plight. J. began where he left off with a fight in the house, after telling me of an accident to a cousin. Again, the boys won. When this was commented on, they were changed to robbers. Superbaby flew and then died. All the dolls committed suicide because they did not have anything. The boy was supreme, but the dog ended up with the house, leaving the boy to sneak back in. There was much concern over the family's deprivation and over whether there would be enough to eat.

J. began to tell me of a hobby of painting ceramic figures. He looked around the office, noticing features of the office for the first time. He asked for permission to play with the objects on my desk. He played that the "chickie eats the tree paper weight," and we discussed his hunger because of the missed sessions. He said "the chickie tries to eat the frog's flowers and W.C. Fields protects the frog." The sink was admired again, but he wanted one of his own, a modern one, when he grows up (i.e., a boy's) and he denigrated something a girl had embroidered for me. He was beginning to think of growing up and leaving therapy and being smart—tomorrow. He concentrated on games of skill with me, basketball in the wastebasket. I noted, 4 months into treatment, that the pressure of speech was off.

At this time, his previous therapist, who had taught him the squiggle drawing game, re-entered the picture. J. drew a lifeguard on a water toy, but he denied missing his previous therapist. Instead, he again began to idealize the sink, but with a difference. He taught me about the pressure in the pipes. He talked of his competent uncle, who is a pipe fitter and has "a very big job putting pipe in a hospital." He corrected me as to the composition of the sink. I was beginning to be somewhat deidealized when I try to focus on his loss of the first therapist. He followed, during the next session, by making a "hot rod monster" driving a car. He was getting in touch with the anger underlying the helplessness and more omnipotent wishes. This was also the week, however, that he was joining the Boy Scouts. But he was very worried about the financial precariousness of his family. J. denied this, covering this up, and covering up errors on his paper with correction fluid. He went on to talk about his father's mechanic activities, and contrasted this with another uncle, who had graduated from college and was able to get any job he wanted. He was working on his cognitive discrepancies concerning the idealized father who was now out of work. He drew a picture of a "monster car" that would not work.

J. dealt with his anger over the potential loss of his dog, who chewed up the furniture. He used police as agents to control his rage in his play. He talked of the bad events of the year and could master this best when he was most idealizing of the therapist. He also talked of his powerful father, who broke both arms of a man who had stolen some car parts. "You better listen when he says something." He denied being worried: "He has the arms, the legs, and the nose." He sang in the next session about all the shortages in America, but "we are going to make it." He put a man back together with glue.

Six months into treatment, J. was sleeping with his brother but still had to be forced to take a bath. He was still fighting with his brother and aggravating his parents. The fears had largely diminished, and he was no longer talking about being ill. The family was cautioned that he was now feeling less ill, but more aggressive, and the importance of limit setting was stressed. J. was flooded with aggressive fantasy just before my 2-week vacation, and this flurry of anger continued briefly on my return.

On my return, J. expressed an interest in skill activities. We played basketball with many compliments for the therapist's playing. He included his brother in the play, but he treated him jealously and roughly. He threatened him with a spanking by mother if he did not behave. He also continued to work on his identification with his father. Before a second vacation, he typed: "Yesterday M. [his dog] ran after a little girl. . . . She was scared and started to scream. She must have really been frightened of my friendly pooch. I wish I knew why she was so scared of my dog. M. wouldn't have bitten her. But she was running and she fell and M. quit chasing her." He seemed to be expressing his concern that his anger was driving the therapist away.

On my return from vacation, he was again talking of his father's great prowess at fixing up cars; at the same time, that he felt that he should be able to dive, but he could not until he was able to swim better. He contrasted his father's adequacy with his own feelings of inadequacy. And the metaphor may be that he still needed help in treatment in order to learn to "swim better." He talked, during the next session, about his spooky fears and of being sucked into the current when swimming in the ocean at Disneyland. Just before my next break, he talked of superheroes and of food. His grandmother cooked the best. And cars—he would probably have a better type car by the time he grew up. In July of that year, just before I went on vacation, he asked whether I was one of those people who stayed in the clinic for only 3 years. He clapped his hands when I said that I was not. He talked after vacation about having missed me, thinking that I would never come back. He said he would see me the next time and the next time, forever.

The next phase of treatment might be called the superhero phase, 9 months into treatment. He began by talking of his broken superheroes and of smashing his old motorcycle. He drew Hulk, strong, powerful, and dumb. He's a Jr., and wouldn't it be funny if someday he was a movie star and someone introduced him as Jr. like Sammy Davis Jr.? He asked of my name and then of many details of my life, the house I lived in, whether I had children, and so forth. The idealizing relationship was holding, and the fear of damage and of underlying helplessness was exposed with the defensive identification with omnipotent (but dumb) superheroes. And he had grandiose fantasies of someday becoming great, powerful, and famous. I gave him a Superman doll for his birthday. He was beginning to sleep in his own bed, and we talked about his fears of growing up. This was followed by a session of ball, in which he needed to have me win. He also told of age-appropriate activities, bowling, and Scouts. He had three badges, Citizen, Athlete, and Engineer. He again talked of his father's adequacy. "But 4 weeks ago I was 9. I want to be 9." "You're an ugly rotten year older. I don't want to be older. I can't watch cartoons, go to school, have to get a yukky job."

Because of his father's new job, several appointments were missed, and J. recapitulated earlier sessions with regressive return to superhero Evel Knieval and aggressive fantasies of shooting him if he failed to jump over snakes. He began to be very concerned about the potential for accident on his father's new job, but his father was reinstated as an idealized object with his new employment.

A new interest in babies cropped up at the birth of his cousin. He believed that God brings babies, and I explained reproduction to him. He wanted his parents to have a baby. I gave him a Spiderman doll for Christmas, remaining with the superheroes. He told me that the three most powerful dolls, in order, were Hulk, Thor, and then Spiderman. Spiderman got into fights but couldn't beat Hulk or Thor. Spiderman did a lot of flying. I was to fly to Florida and be away one session. He brought Hulk and Spiderman to the next session, and they fought and flew. He admitted he had been afraid that my plane would crash. He missed a session because of illness. We talked of how he used to be nervous but was no longer nervous and of the fact that he now only occasionally had headaches.

The next phase of treatment might be the shift from interest only in the omnipotence of superheroes to collecting. He collected dolls and comic books. He counted the latter, read them, and brought them in to show me. At about this time, I saw his parents, who would be terminating their own treatment soon. His mother focused on J.'s agitation and on the waxing and waning of his fears. He had to be walked to the bathroom or bedroom by his brother, and there was increased fighting with his brother and other children: "He wants them to look up to him and consider him the greatest, even though, he fights with them. They refused to play with him, but they always came back; he was fairly popular."

J. was uncomfortable the next session, when I could not figure out how to use the manual calculator (deidealization). He resorted to magic and Martian clay figures. Then he said that computers can only give answers, but we can walk and talk and think and give answers. We played with fashioned computers from objects on the desk. Our robots provided each other with protection, and our computers needed to be very powerful to protect us from the bad guys and to feed us.

His great grandmother died. He mastered the pencil sharpener and the calculator and talked of the evanescence of life: "Why can't people live forever?" And that nobody is perfect, as we play ball. A subsequent session was spent playing hide and seek (looking for the lost object). The king had a crown that is the symbol of his power, and the lion paperweight was called glue. J. was concerned with my plants living and being cared for. We continued the game between the computer and the king. The king's bodyguard and the computer fought. Later, the lion became the king of the friends rather than the king of the beasts. J. drew pictures that he hung on my wall. He remembered the rooms in which he used to see his previous therapist. He played with the Great Kitten that was going to save the world. When we played basketball,the little cat bookmark he was calling the Great Kitten fell in a hole in the side of the desk. He was very upset, tried to get it out, and said his father could get the desk panel off to obtain it.

Sixteen months into treatment, the parents reported that J. was goofing off at school and at Sunday School and that he lacked consideration for others. He was bothering his brother. I talked with the parents about using fewer threats and more consistent methods of limit setting, with rewards for good behavior. His great grandmother had died, and he was not talking about it at home. Also, his uncle attempted suicide. J. was told that he had had an operation. The uncle later succeeded in committing suicide. His grandmother was in the hospital at that time.

J. and I talked of his goofing off and distracting other children. He talked of his getting his work done early because he was smarter—why were other children so slow? This was followed by more description of Evel Knieval jumping hurdles, but he was able to discuss what he could do at school instead when he finished his work early so that he does not distract the rest of the class. He was temporarily upset with the criticism. He said he played space man with his previous therapist, so we played space man. We lived increasing lengths of time on the moon and got huge quantities of food. This was followed by a warm session, in which we discussed nicknames and he gave me one. He talked of his great grandmother's death and how now he will never learn (language) from her. Next session he talked of his uncle's death from suicide. Everyone has to die, but now he would never get to the place his uncle was going to take him where they make comic books. He wanted me to come and visit his home. He continued to mourn his uncle. He tried to get me to see his aunt, and he told me he would like to come see me throughout his whole life. He was not as nervous as he had been; he was still nervous, but not as earlier.

During the next session, he was very angry about my forthcoming vacation. He told me that I was a better doctor than his previous one and I was nicer. Then he said he used to be very nervous and now he was not. I asked about fears, and he said he used to be afraid, he doesn't remember what he used to be afraid of. He couldn't watch Frankenstein movies, and he was afraid of those, but he couldn't remember the other things he was afraid of. He followed this by drawing a powerful Magna tank ray gun and one not as strong. When it was interpreted that he needed protection, he said no, he was strong. We worked on my vacation and the therapy loss, and he went to the moon again. He came back after discussion of the break and when I promised to bring him a comic book. He was bitten by a dog in my absence, and he was very worried about his father's taking some junk that had fallen off a truck. He brought in his comic book collection to show me. He was jealous of all the birthday gifts his brother got. Now he stated he wanted to grow up so he could do more things. But he was also afraid of going on some of the rides at Great America, but then he would feel sorry if he did not. He brought in a plant for my birthday. We always planted or talked about growing things when he was grieving over loss. Maybe I would see the comic book factory when I went East on my vacation. He was concerned that my plane would be hijacked. He then talked of a baby who needed rescuing but became superbaby, doing many dangerous things. We talked of superheroes and helplessness, but now the superbaby was powerful. This was tied to his feeling helpless when I went on vacation, and he wished he were powerful. He said that he did not feel so powerful. I brought him a comic book from my vacation. On my return, he told of all his activities and that he had gone on the rides at Great America.

His mother thought she was pregnant but, when I returned from vacation, it turned out not to be the case. J. drew pictures of babies and said he loved babies. He talked of being nervous while I had been away. He saw a man knocked down while changing a tire. He was nervous riding on his cousin's motorcycle, and there was a big dog when he got off, and he had a nervous stomach ache. He was afraid I would not be in that day and that he would be unable to talk about this. We needed a special telephone or CB to keep in communication. Subsequent sessions he asked to use the tape recorder. He talked of how strange he sounded to himself. He talked of how he would miss his brother if something happened to him, after dreaming that he was shot, and he talked of feeling much better.

Next, I was told that J. was flunking school because he was not getting his work in. J. was scared after my brief hospitalization. He was able to talk of his having been bitten by a dog, of his grandparent's death, and of the death of his uncle. He was afraid he would have to go back to his previous doctor, whom he never liked. He said he had told this doctor a dream about becoming witches, stealing food, and then finding gold behind the rainbow to pay for the hotdogs so they wouldn't be stealing, and that all the doctor said was that it must be because it was Halloween. We talked of his schoolwork. He said children were stealing it. I told him he was not helpless, that he could lock it up in his locker. He told me he never got to show his previous doctor his coin collection, after he expressed concern that perhaps I would die.

J. was then able to tell me that he had been able to stay up all night when he was sick and vomiting without being afraid or calling his parents. He used to be afraid that he would die when that used to happen. He looked at my coin collection, having forgotten his, and selected the next best coin to keep. Next week he brought in his coin collection. He gave me a jewelry box for Christmas after much trouble deciding what to give me and what to give others. His mother asked to see me; J.'s idea was that it was over his fighting with his brother. He announced that he was not as interested in comic books or science fiction as he used to be. He liked things now that are more real. But he still liked the superhero ones, telling me a violent Batman story.

His mother told me she wanted to see me, not to tell me how badly J. was doing, but to tell me how *well* he was doing. He had gone into a slump in schoolwork at the beginning of the year. She and his teacher decided that it was a depression over his uncle's death. He talked about it incessantly just after it happened. But at this time, his schoolwork had picked up, his report card was very good, and she felt he had improved with me. She felt he had been on a plateau with the previous doctor but perhaps he would have gotten worse if they had taken him out of treatment with him.

J. played train with me, the train saved someone; he also talked of being good at football. He told me of being put on skates when he was 3 years old, being blown by the wind. I asked if it had made him feel helpless. No, he felt like he was flying. During the next session, when we discussed an absence because of his mother's becoming ill, he told me that he felt nervous and crummy when he did not come in. He remembered the various games we played together; he then played basketball and let me win. He told me that I was the best baseball player: would we play in the Spring?

At this time in his treatment, now of 3 years duration, J.'s mother became ill and had to be hospitalized. He was able to express his nervousness about her being ill and to deal with this worry directly. When I made a robot for him out of clay after he had drawn cartoons, including Jiminy Cricket, he said that the robot was sick. He also talked during the next session about murderous relatives and began to express in this way his concern that her illness might be hereditary. There was a return to the grandiose defense in his behavior.

He told of having been hit by a bike and of almost being wiped out. When this was related to his mother's illness, he could express his anger more directly about the vague promises that his mother would be coming home soon, as well as his helplessness in the face of her illness and his feeling that she was not trying. He turned to reality problems: difficulty with math. A vacation brought a return of more grandiose fantasy and a remembering of some of the things we had done in previous sessions. It also brought nervousness and worry again that my plane might crash or disappear as in the Bermuda triangle.

J. began to be interested in sessions following this vacation with reality concerns: his science project at school, becoming a football player. There was more concern with doing things that would build his self-esteem. I quote from the notes at this time: "I sense that there is a need to separate, and a dreaming of aggrandizement, but in much more realistic terms than his usual identification with superheroes, and a beginning interest in girls." He had previously asked about my religion during Easter, and we had compared notes about our different religions, a beginning distancing from the transference and introduction of more reality in the relationship. After this vacation, I sensed some distance from me without being anxious, and we talked of realistic ways of increasing his self-esteem.

It was interesting that after what seemed to be a movement toward separation and reality, he returned to play with the clay figures about powerful figures. He had seen a strong man on TV who killed a girl because she was teasing him. He asked to take out his clay figures and proceeded to stab his monster, which he had worked so hard to create, with my letter opener. He remade the monster into a strong man with lots of muscles. He directed me to make a strong man of my own and made sure to give me more clay to make him larger. He said that it was the metal in him that made him vulnerable: "With that metal in him, he will live forever." He wrestled with the missile and destroyed the missile, but his legs got weak. He said then that he was falling off a cliff and that the only way to kill him was to drop a penny on him, which would split him in half. I thought at the time that he was continuing to be concerned about his uncle's suicide and may have been referring to his belief that he could not have drowned as he was such a strong swimmer. I was puzzled at this regression: Was it mother's illness and return home? Or my brief vacation? On retrospect, perhaps his brief flight into health and individuation was frightening to him at the time of her illness.

The play with the clay figures continued. He asked me to make a road like his; I said I had made a drawbridge. We made castles, and he liked my castle better than his. I said that our castles did not have to look exactly like each other's, that we were different, and if they were exactly the same we wouldn't know whose was whose. His missile burned up the road, and the king put the missile in chains until he was better and then gave him castor oil. We talked of how terrible that tasted, and he said that was what his grandmother used to give him when he was sick, and he got better right away. So the missile got better, but this time it knocked over the TV set, missing the castle. He rebuilt the missile and the castle so that it would rebound off the castle. The missile was so powerful and strong it could cut through diamonds like glass. They were afraid that the missile would go out of control. But then the missile saved the king, and the king saved the missile because he liked him.

He continued this play in the next session. He reminded me that they were about to destroy the kingdom, which he did, but the muscle man fixed everything up. Many battles ensued between the space parasite and the muscle man. When he finally killed him, he was brought back to life by the radiation box. However, muscle man turned on them, because something had happened to his brain, and he went up to the sun to get the radiation out of head. He burnt to a crisp but miraculously came back to life and was rebuilt stronger than ever, so powerful it would take a jet going 2500 miles per hour to destroy him again. He flattened the muscle man's head, calling him a monster when his head was injured, and talked about his melting in water. He told me about his father melting iron in acid. I wondered whether the reference to the injured brain that made muscle man into a monster referred to his mother's illness, although this speculation was kept to myself. In the next session, this play continued, but he called our figures "brothers." Each one was interviewed to see who was the strongest. He was concerned during these games with who was winning. He said that in real life he liked to win, but this was just pretend so we would let them take turns. He said that he did that with his brother. In a later session, he made rules about who was the winner and who the loser, and he noticed paintings and certificates in the office. He talked of medals he had won. We had by this time named our clay figures the Masked Marvel (his) and the Jolly Green Giant (mine).

His man gradually evolved into a soldier, whom he renamed Hermy the Robot, and he talked of the soldiers being bored, as the war had gone on for 8 years. He also said that he was tired of wrestling, and I said I had noticed he did not do it this day. He said: "Yes. It destroys his man and it gets soft and too hard to fix up." He returned to playing with the sink, much as in earlier sessions. My comment to myself at this time was: "So the wrestling is getting 'boring.' Is he talking about a sense that therapy is coming to an end? Clearly, he has worked from superfigures to figures closer to reality, which is a sign he is moving toward later latency preoccupations."

My hunch seemed correct, because subsequent sessions dealt with reality interests, such as going to a baseball game and about a friend who was trying out to be bat boy, something he did subsequently. He approached this with some grandiosity. He wanted to grow up and make a lot of money at something that is easy, so he thinks he'll be a ball player, he has to work at his hits. About this time, he told a religious joke involving the religion I had told him I belonged to. My understanding of this was that it was a further distancing from me and beginning deidealization, which would help him with separation and termination. My upcoming vacation reminded him of his previous look at his chart, and he noted that his drawings now looked much different from those that he had drawn for his previous therapist. He was measuring his own progress. He talked of an injury to his nail and, subsequent to my vacation, he began to talk of his fears of being hurt playing football. He said that he had mixed feelings about the football team. But his father wanted him to be in all of these things, football, baseball, karate, boxing. He was frightened of football, particularly of boxing. He spoke about a football player whose face was crushed and of injuries in boxing. His father wanted him to do all the things he never got to do. He then began to talk of his other fears. He wondered whether it was normal to be frightened. He spoke of being frightened of the dark, and he was afraid to sleep over someone's house. He traced this to when he was 6 years old and slept at an aunt's house, and the kids took him down to the basement and scared him. Since this time he had slept overnight only once, 1 year earlier. He talked of being sick sleeping at his grandmother's house—dizzy and sick to his stomach. They thought he had stomach flu and his mother took his temperature next morning and he was fine. There were two things he reported being frightened of. First, kids picking on him—he had told earlier of kids picking on him in the park, and he pretend-cried to get out of it. What if those two kids were on a team; he had no idea. His second fear was sleeping over someone's house (but you don't have to do this if you don't want to). Could I help him with these fears? I suggested that he might be more frightened today because of my going on vacation, but yes, we could talk about those things.

After this vacation, there was continued discussion of his fears about continuing with football and about the loss of

Elvis. He did some soothing of his self-esteem, saying that he played football well with friends, even though he was contemplating getting off the football team. Clay play moved to making baseball figures of players he admired, and he brought in a book of baseball feats, which he read to me. He had not decided whether to continue to try out for the teams, but he openly worried about whether he would be any good. He finally began to be able to separate sufficiently that when he was in a play, he asked to leave a session early to make a rehearsal.

J. came in and played with the clay figures, saying that we hadn't played with them in a long time. He complained about the clay, saying that the clay pieces melted at school. I commented that it doesn't last forever and asked whether he thought things should last forever. He agreed that they couldn't. I wondered whether he thought he would be coming to our sessions forever. He said no, it had to stop sometime—when would it stop? I asked whether he was nervous and how school was going. He said no, he wasn't nervous, he was doing well in school, although not great in English. How would we decide when he should stop? I said again that it depended on whether he was nervous and whether things were going well in school. He wondered whether he could stop for awhile, and see—and then would we know? I asked whether he had thought of this before, and he said suddenly, yes he had, but then his mother got sick and he got nervous. I said that what we could do then was to meet every other week for awhile, and then once a month to see whether he got nervous. He said he would like to try in 2 weeks. The rest of this session was reality oriented and scientific, with none of the pressured speech or affect noted at the beginning of treatment, and little nervousness about discussing termination.

He talked differently about his nervousness during the next session. He was afraid to go to the board or to give oral presentations, but he told himself he was going to do it and to get an A, and he did it, even though he was afraid he would mess up. We talked more about his fears of death and of the losses in his life and of his fears of sleeping at other people's houses. This material was reworked in several of the termination sessions. He agreed that it was related to his fear that his family would not be there when he returned. He was then able to relate his fears of not doing well in sports to his short height. He had become able to examine his fears and to trace the genetic origins of his fears. We were then able to make our appointments once a month, for two appointments, and then in 2-month follow-up appointments, and a 3-month follow-up appointment. Since the termination, I have not heard from him or his parents.

Kohut (1983, p. 4) indicated that the "spontaneous establishment of one of the stable narcissistic transferences is the best and most reliable diagnostic sign which differentiates these patients from psychotic or borderline cases, on the one hand, and from ordinary transference neuroses, on the other." From almost the first four sessions, this child established an idealizing transference with the therapist. He also at times related in a twinning fashion with her. One can see from the foregoing description of the treatment process how he then explored and worked through the grandiosity of the grandiose self and brought it into alignment with reality. He moved from identifications with grandiose and superheroes to a more realistic appraisal of the self. He could then also deal with his own helplessness and vulnerabilities and deal directly with the fears and symptoms that had brought him into treatment. He was almost able to separate at the time of his mother's illness. However, her illness brought about a regression and re-exploration of his omnipotent fantasies and rage. However, it provided him with an opportunity to deal with his rage at her vulnerability and accompanying inaccessibility to him. He was able to explore his parental representations and to bring them more in line with reality. He was then able to reappraise the therapist, deidealize her, and finally separate from her.

9

TREATMENT OF NEUROTIC CHILDREN

The presence of psychoneurosis in childhood as well as at older ages is characterized by conflict, anxiety, and higher-level ego defenses. The major characteristic of the conflict is that it is not with the environment, but with an internalized conflict. The conflict may have originated with the environment, that is, with parental figures. For it to characterize a neurotic conflict, it must now be internalized within the personality of the child. Just as an adult, a child may have a psychoneurotic personality organization, without overt symptoms, in times of least stress. The child may become symptomatic at times of stress, relating either to increased impulse life, increased superego pressures, or increased environmental pressures. The fluctuating quality of the child's behavior and symptoms may also relate to the fluctuation of maturational pressures. Also, as development progresses, the child may have an opportunity to rework earlier developmental issues, hence may "outgrow" the neurotic organizational structure. Thus, psychoneurosis in childhood has a relatively good prognosis, within a benign environment with or without treatment.

The major components of a psychoneurosis are those of conflict and anxiety, which generate symptoms when the stressors are great or the defenses insufficient to bind the anxiety. The other characteristic is that the conflict is not only an internal one but is unconscious. That is, the child is unaware of the underlying motivators or of aspects of the conflict. He chooses to be unaware of them, because to know would be to suffer intense anxieties about either the forbidden aspects of the conflict or fear of punishment for the forbidden wishes or impulses. The source of these impulses in a neurosis is generally believed to be either aggressive or sexual wishes or impulses. The child buries these forbidden wishes about which he is in conflict, and remains unaware or unconscious of them. He uses various defensive devices to ward off knowing about them. Like in the dream, associations or memories related to these unconscious feelings, impulses, wishes, or conflicts about their expression may be distantly related to the original conflict. Symptoms that result from the anxiety about the conflict may also be derivatives or compromise formations relating to the conflict.

The nodal points for psychoneurosis are pure anxiety states, anxiety hysterias, obsessive-compulsive neuroses, and conversion hysterias. We may also see character-disorder formation with neurotic overlays or behavior disorders that are neurotically motivated. For treatment, the difference in approach will be determined by a recognition of the different types of defense associated with these types. For anxiety hysterias, the major mechanisms are displacement and projection toward the formation of the phobias. The major mechanisms in the conversions are repression or more severe dissociative splits. And the obsessive-compulsive child may use a variety of mechanisms, including doing/undoing, reaction formation, isolation, and intellectualization. The pure anxiety state has fewer defenses with which to cope.

Play has been said to be the language of childhood. Play and play-action methods are ideally suited to the treatment of children with neurotic disorders. Highly verbal neurotic children with good secondary process thinking and observing egos can be approached directly with verbal therapy techniques. Even in some of these children, however, blocks and disruptions in the therapy process may be overcome with play methods as association devices. The content and symbolism of the play may help trace the connections to the forbidden fears and wishes, "the royal road to the unconscious." When these have been traced, the conflicts can be more overtly discussed in verbal terms and with secondary process thinking.

As with many disorders of childhood, there is reluctance to diagnose psychoneurosis in children before there is much personality structure, that is, before the age of 6. This relates to the belief that more structure needs to be present for conflict and superego pressures to be at work. There is some agreement that precursors to neurotic behaviors and symptoms as well as structures may be seen in 3- to 4-year-olds. However, it is important to recognize that even children beyond the age of 6 are in developmental flux and transition; even more crystallized neurotic structures have the opportunity for reorganization beyond that age. Furthermore, the reorganization need not necessarily be in the direction of greater health and normality. Children with beginning development of neurosis may resort to more behavioral symptoms and, without relief from internal and external pressures, may develop a more characterological adaptation. They are less likely to regress further than this, without great stress, because the presumption is that there has been adequate separation and individuation and development of object constancy.

Case Example: J. Jr. The first case to be presented is that of an early separation-anxiety disorder, which might be considered a precursor of neurosis in a girl, aged 3 years, 5 months; she was referred by her grandparents, who at that time were the custodial guardians. She was having behavioral reactions and upset because of a custody battle between her mother and her mother's parents. The pregnancy and delivery were normal, and she lived with her mother and father until 6 months of age. She was often left with other people for caretaking during this period of her life. There would be marital disagreements, and the grandparents would often pick up the child, or the child and her mother. She was with the grandparents from 7 to 10 months of age. She returned to her parents between 10 months and 1 year of age but spent every weekend with her grandparents. She lost weight and became withdrawn and lethargic. She would run all over the house to seek a familiar place. There were many fights at home, and the grandparents did not know whether she had been abused. She would sit up in her crib and rock, saying, "bad girl, bad girl." She did not sleep well at her grandparents' house although her mother said she always slept well. At 1 year of age, the mother brought the child to the grandparents and agreed to give them legal custody. Legal custody was obtained when J. Jr. was 13 months old.

At this time, the child was petrified to be picked up; she kept repeating "bad girl." She would wake up at night and would cry for 1–2 hours. There was no eye contact. A psychiatrist said at that time she had been traumatized. Slowly, for the first 6–7 months, the grandparents had to take turns waking her and bringing her into contact. She now woke up momentarily at times of stress. She would be courteous to mother when she visited but would become rigid. She would act out hostility after the visit. She would pull her hair and hit her head and then give affection. Recently she had started biting her finger and to cry. She bit her grandfather on the arm. There was also a lot of aggressive play with a teddy bear and with a doll family of grandmother and grandfather and child. Others would come and take the child away.

At the time of referral, her physical health was good, after a bout of the flu, for which she needed to be hospitalized with IV tubes. Her grandmother stayed with her in the hospital for 5 days. She had had German measles at the time she began to walk, at about 8 months. She talked at 10½ months, in sentences at 14–15 months. She trained herself to the potty at 27 months. She did not stay with mother since the legal custody, and she was left alone with her uncle, a teenager, for periods of only an hour and a half. Her mother had not been to visit, and there was no physical contact during her earlier visits. Her mother is now pregnant and is warmer and more ingratiating. She was remarried, when J. Jr. was about 22 months old, and she was angry that the grandparents did not come to the wedding. J. Jr.'s father visits with her and treats her with warmth and kindness.

J. Jr. was examined initially with the Draw A Person Test, the Stanford Binet, Form L-M Intelligence test, the Rorschach, and a diagnostic play session. She obtained an IQ of 140 on the Binet and a standard score of 96 on her human figure drawing. The Rorschach agreed with her intellectual level, in that there were two human figures in the protocol, which was advanced for her chronological age level. The rest of the record, however, indicated fears (bats and spiders) and depression (preoccupation with the color black). She also had difficulty seeing color, the presence of which is expected in her age range, and her accuracy level was low (30%).

It became clearer in the play session as to what was making the child tense and fearful. She expressed concern about whether she was going home and asked several times where I worked. For much of the diagnostic, she could not be seen alone, although the play session was with her alone. She brought all her toys into the session and then carefully packed them to go while I saw her grandparents. She told me:

> I don't want to go away with my mommy and B. [the new stepfather]. I want to stay with grandmother until I'm bigger. I go out and take them somewhere to jail because I don't want to go with them. Sometimes I dream scary dreams and I cry because I won't go with my mommy and B. I don't like anybody. I don't like mommy and B. because they want to take me.

THE TREATMENT PROCESS

J. Jr. was seen for almost exactly 1 year in once-weekly treatment, with the grandparents being seen as well approximately once monthly. The first treatment session proper was about a month after the initial diagnostic evaluation. The issues of both the first and second treatment sessions, a week apart, were whether she was going to stay and whether she was going to be parted from grandmother. Grandmother did come into the sessions with us. The coping strategy she seemed to be using was to maintain sameness. She had dolls like those of mine. She wanted to play with the "toys" (tests) she had played with during the diagnostic. She put a puzzle together that was similar to one we had done then. When she played ring toss, the colors of the rings had to match the dolls on the ring-toss base. She generally explored the playroom, fingering many objects and dumping others out. She commented that there were too many toys. She expressed some anger with an alligator puppet, which she had bite me in play with its jaws. My impression after the first session was that she was used to manipulating her grandparents. Her grandfather informed me that J. Jr. had been playing with dolls and had shown baby being taken away and crying. I assured him at this time that she would get to material of this sort after we had gotten to know each other.

During the second testing session, J. Jr. tried to manipulate me by demanding that I take her outside so she could use her roller skates. There was more exploratory play with many materials, including the schoolhouse and puppets, as well as questions about the toys, but also about me. When I answered her that I worked in a hospital, she decided she also wanted to work in a hospital. I felt that this was another coping device; she could feel more secure if she were doing exactly as I did, twinned or merged. At the end of this session, the grandfather reported that new symptoms had emerged. She was not playing as well with her friends, she couldn't stand up for herself, and she seemed to be withdrawing from them. She was having to be carried when they went shopping, she was having many aches and pains and headaches, and she could not let her grandmother out of her sight. I was having some questions about the level of generation differentiation in the family, as grandmother, mother, and J. Jr. had the same first name. The adaptation to this was to call the child's mother and J. Jr. by their middle names.

By the third session, she was continuing to ask to have her grandmother accompany her, but with a difference. Grandmother was not included in the play, and she could slip away much more quickly to the front room, where she would read along with grandfather. J. Jr. informed me rather quickly during this session about a new event that was preoccupying her. She opened the doll house, commented on the baby buggy, and told me that her mother and stepfather were going to have a baby. She commented on the playpen and the baby bed. I asked whether they were going to use hers, and she said that she had her own playpen. She fled to other play with the nerf plane that had a weight in it. She had played with this previously, at one point aggressively throwing it at me. She moved quickly from toy to toy, plane–wooden truck–wooden paddle boat–toy guitar, which needed mending, and drawing letters on the blackboard of the schoolhouse. She became very concerned with chalk on the floor and the need to clean it, although in earlier sessions she had refused to help put toys away. She got close enough to finger my hands, which had chalk and ink on them. She began to use devices to stay longer (e.g., stacking the train parts).

A month into treatment, J. Jr. began to form an attachment to me. Her grandfather informed me at the beginning of the fourth treatment session that she had been asking all week after me, and wanted to know what I did. She was told that I help children with their fears. She asked what a psychologist was, where I worked, and whether she could visit me there. I felt forced to tell the grandparents, and later her during the session, that in 2 weeks I would be taking a 2-week vacation. She then needed both grandparents to accompany her in this session, but after two rounds of ring toss she could allow the grandfather to return to the front room and, almost immediately, the grandmother. Most of the session was spent in writing letters on the chalkboard, with the difference that she would now allow me to write some and to teach her some. She also initiated a tea party with the new tea set. She was upset that one meeting had to be changed because of a trip the family was planning to a farm. Her anger was expressed more overtly to me by putting chalk on the floor, on both our hands, on my arm, and getting it very close to my dress. The grandparents were to see me for a session. They both wanted answers to questions. The grandmother wanted to know how I knew that it was not she who had caused the problems, and the grandfather wanted to know how to handle her when they set limits and she became enraged. In the past, she has bitten him, and she was now biting herself.

During the grandparents' session, I began by answering their questions. I explained that J. Jr.'s disturbance evolved from the many uprootings in her early life, which had interfered with bonding, and that, as her grandfather had put it, there was a lack of trust. I put her emotionally at the level of a 2-year-old, in the throes of asserting herself and her independence, expressing rage at having this interfered with, and a need for a controlling omnipotent defense. Her grandfather then wanted help with her rage at their setting limits. I asked for some examples that we could talk about. Her grandmother gave the example of J. Jr. drumming, this getting out of hand, and of ending in her hitting the cat. She would tell her to stop, the child would hit the cat again, and then, when grandmother attempted to get the stick out of her hand, she would hit grandmother. We were talking then about not letting things escalate, perhaps taking the stick before she hit the cat and perhaps also anticipating her getting overexcited and distracting her with some new activity. The grandmother said that she knew all this intellectually but that she lets it escalate before she acts, then gets angry herself. The grandfather gave the example of tickling her, and she would start biting his pajamas. He would be called to the phone, and she would bite him. He would then tell her that it makes him very sad when she does this. I said that in addition to her being age 2 emotionally and age 5 intellectually, she is going into the phallic phase, and one has to be careful not to overstimulate her. I would have stopped the tickling when she began to bite his pajamas, again anticipating when she gets overloaded, and interrupting the activity then. We agreed that she does need some physical contact but that there is a fine line to overstimulation. Both grandparents understood what I was saying—their need to act as her stimulus barrier. The grandparents felt her recent clinging to them during the session as representing fear of loss of the old object as she got tied to the new object.

Other issues concerning the grandparents were then reviewed, as well as the behaviors the child had exhibited when they first obtained guardianship and the status of the court fight for custody. The court said that they wished to see how the mother did with the new baby before making a decision. The grandparents were worried that the stepfather's rough children would be visiting next winter.

The session before my vacation began with many limits set. J. Jr. brought a basket, flashlight, and grandmother's stool with her. She began by bringing her grandparents with her and playing briefly with them. She asked what was outside the door; when she was told it was a porch, she asked to see the porch and, spotting a yard and a jungle gym in the next yard, she wanted to go down. When refused, she was angry and left me to go to see her grandparents. She returned to play having a tea party for "a friend" who later couldn't leave her baby. She had difficulty naming a puppet mommy, then decided it was a daddy, and she named a boy and a girl, looking at her genitals. The Frankenstein doll was named a mommy. The alligator puppet was again used to bite me all over; when I said it was biting me on the arm, where she had bitten the grandfather, she looked distressed, bent over, and immediately fled to the chest of toys. Time was up, and she had to be reminded that next week she was going to the farm with her grandparents. She seemed to be concerned as to whether she would return; she said that she had not yet played with a blond doll and that she had not put the toys away. Some guilt about not helping seemed to be re-emerging with the realization of a separation.

There was almost a month's break in the treatment because of a vacation. The first session after this, the grandparents informed me that the child's mother had given up her suit for custody of J. Jr. Because of this information, the grandparents, J. Jr., and I sat down to discuss the implications of this change. The grandparents informed me that the daughter felt that her situation was unstable because of problems in her new marriage. A divorce was not imminent, as the husband did not want to divorce after less than 1 year of marriage and with his wife pregnant. The grandparents felt that the child's mother now thought she might need the grandparents' support in the future. I asked J. Jr. whether she understood that she need not fear now that she would be removed from the grandparents, as her mother had told her she could stay with them as long as she wanted. She whistled to indicate that she understood. I then asked whether the grandparents wanted me to continue to see the child. They said yes, until she became more stable. The grandfather reported that she was ill in the middle of the week and that she was crying as she used to when she had first come to them. The grandfather also reported that J. Jr. had asked for me frequently. I agreed to continue treating her and said that we would meet in the near future to discuss what had been going on and where we would be headed in the future treatment.

The shorter session with J. Jr. began with her being able to go immediately to the playroom without asking either grandparent to come along. I had a surprise of a Beatrix Potter book, and we began by reading that. She also played with new puzzles I had obtained on my trip. I asked her whether she now understood that she would be remaining with the grandparents and whether she would like to continue seeing me. After a lengthy pause and several repetitions of the question, she said yes. We continued to play, this time with a domino game. And she picked up a gun and asked where the caps were. I said I didn't believe in caps for boys and girls, but that the gun did make a sound. She told me she knew someone who did have something to go in a gun. When I told her time was up, she asked about the toy snake I had brought from vacation (a very large and long snake). She asked where the mouth was. She made a game out of getting me, similar to what she had previously done with the alligator puppet.

After this session, the grandmother told me that J. Jr. was uptight with the judge when he explained the decision, and the grandfather said she had seemed to be disconnected and did not seem to be listening. The grandmother felt that she was still worried, so I said it is as if she didn't believe it and that at her age who could blame her. When I explained to J. Jr. a change in appointment that would mean her coming in earlier, she said that she slept late. I said it would still be in the afternoon, and she again teased with a big smile on her face that she slept all day. She appeared to have counted on the relationship with me and had developed some trust in me but was not completely trusting of the judge's decision.

The following session was a calm one, in which J. Jr. seemed to be exploring the other materials in the playroom and making certain that she would be coming to see me. It seemed very important to her that I be paying attention to her. I kept fewer materials available, since too many had seemed to be overstimulating to her previously. I made a rule that she finish with one toy before going on to the next, to provide further structure for her. The grandparents and I agreed that J. Jr. seemed calmer today because she felt assured that she would be continuing to see me and that she would be staying with them and probably that seeing me did not mean she would be leaving them.

During the session with the grandparents, they reported again that this had been a calm week but that yesterday J. Jr. had been anxious again. The grandmother reported two events that had upset her. One had been J. Jr. finding that her grandmother had given some of her baby things to her mother for the expected new baby. The grandmother had reassured J. Jr. that she was not giving away her bed and that in future she would ask her about anything she planned to give away before she did so. The other event was that the natural father had visited with a youngster of her own age. The grandfather felt that J. Jr. was jealous of the attention given this child, although she later played well with the child. We agreed that she might be feeling displaced by the expected new baby, even though she did not want to live with her mother. We also discussed J. Jr.'s recent questioning of why she needed to come to see me, since it was earlier tied to the custody battle. She was told that she was coming now to help her become happier inside.

The grandmother had asked why it was that whereas J. Jr. used to be almost too friendly with strangers, she tended to be withdrawn and oppositional now when she was anxious. I explained this in terms of a defensive strategy. In earlier sessions, the rage had broken through with the alligator puppet, the snake (about which she became concerned when I taped up nails that stuck out of it), and the gun. I now began to see more overt oppositionality. She threw her jacket on the floor and understood that that is not where jackets are placed. She said that they go in the closet. When it was suggested she place the jacket on a chair, she put it on the table. She played well with many toys and asked about many toys. However, the relationship itself seemed to have much meaning for her. She began asking about how long we would have to spend together during a session, asked to stay longer in the session, and wondered where I lived and she lived. She said that she would like me to live next to her room. She showed some jealousy of my relationship with the grandparents. When her grandfather told a joke and the adults laughed, I commented that she wanted to understand the joke so that she could laugh. She did two somersaults for us. She was anxious about an upcoming session that would be missed, and her comment was: "You're always gone." I said that it only felt like I was always gone.

The entire following session dealt with her rage at the displacement by the expected new baby. She began with concern as to where people in the doll house were going to sleep. A huge fight ensued between the little girl and the baby about who was going to sleep in the cradle. Once the little girl came looking for the mother as well as the baby. Most of the session was concerned with the little girl stealing into the cradle and the baby being very angry because the little girl was in the bed. She would pound the baby doll up and down on the table. This had started with the boy taking the baby's place on the layette table. The anger crescendoed. Just as suddenly, she became very quiet, and said, "that's weird that the little girl won't let the baby have the bed." She decided to stop playing with the dollhouse. She played with a beach ball and decided to have a tea party. She asked about the Frankenstein doll, and I commented that it was a very scary doll. She parted by shooting me playfully with the gun.

The next session was 2 weeks later, after a week's vacation. There was an undercurrent during this session. J. Jr. came, saying her mouth was mixed up, and I began by saying I would help her unmix it. When I showed her a surprise book, she said that her mouth was unmixed. She played a bit with coloring the book but picked up the Frankenstein doll and asked me to fix its leg, which was off. Then she brought the gun to me and asked about the noise and how each part worked; she said she could make a loud noise. I asked why she wasn't playing with the book—was it because I had been gone? She said she could wait for me. I said that she could wait for me and that I had missed her. She took out the tea set and began to play tea party. She ordered me to pick up something that she had dropped. I said that she could pick it up herself, that she was the one playing with it. She did so. I wondered why she liked to order me around—was it because I had left her? She had also asked how many days I had been gone, but she also said several times, "nothing." She changed the subject rather than listen to any comments about my having been gone. She played a game of having me count the cups and, as she took them away and put them back, she hid the top of the teapot for me to guess what she had in her hand. I commented that she was playing all the things we had done together during the testing session, to remember them. She said yes. She then said there was a little black kitten that was lost. She told me then about their cat Tom, who had died. She went to ask grandfather when Tom had died. I said that was sad. She continued to be concerned about the lost kitten and then denied being sad about Tom. I wondered how she thought the kitten got out. She said it was through the screen, which had fallen out. I later found that it had happened 2 weeks ago and that grandfather had fixed the screen. I said that I hoped somebody would find the kitten, but I thought she might be worried it would die as well. About this time, she was concerned with the tea being all gone. I wondered whether she had been worried about me when I was gone. She said no. We played ring toss, with her winning with made-up high scores, and then played with the toy soldiers. She asked many questions about soldiers and how they protect themselves. "Do they shoot at people sometimes?" She was first going to help me put away the soldiers but later seemed to be about to dump them all out. I suggested we put them all away (to avoid an escalation of anger), and she helped me with this and the ring-toss game. She asked me, at the end of the session, when I would be going away again and when she would see me again. I said I would see her Friday and that I would not be going away again for some time.

A new concern, which now began to alternate with her preoccupation with her new baby sister, was about whether and when she would be going to preschool. It had been suggested to the grandparents that they wait the 6 months after she turned 4 in January, until she had settled down more, before enrolling her in school. She expressed these concerns in the following way. She told me first that she had a baby sister and her name. When asked whether she liked the name, she changed the subject and said that the baby carriage did not belong in the garage. Then she turned to the schoolhouse. She was concerned that there was not a seat for one of the schoolchildren and about where the teacher was. When I found two dolls the same, and said one was the mother doll, first she had me put it back in the house, and then she returned the mother doll to the schoolhouse. She was concerned about the new baby and about where mother would be. She was also concerned as to who would send her to school. She told me over and over again, when I could not understand her speech for the moment, that the granddaughter told the grandmother and/or the grandfather when it was time to go to school. The grandparents also told of a new anxiety that had cropped up at home. She had discovered that her little friends have mothers and fathers, and she was now trying to come to terms with this and was calling the grandmother, mother, and the grandfather, dad. During the next session, she asked about a goodbye drawing on my bulletin board. I answered that it said goodbye but that it did not mean that she was saying goodbye—that she had looked frightened. She asked what happened to the little girl, and I said that she was with her mother and father and happy. She said that grandmothers and grandfathers are mothers and fathers first, and I said yes.

A new theme emerged in our relationship, which now also began to alternate with the themes described earlier. She began first subtly, and eventually overtly, to express her anger and oppositionality. It took the form of kicking me under the table. First she touched my feet and said that the feet were saying hello to each other, but then the feet were fighting with each other, but very playfully. This occurred after a missed session. She asked whether I had missed her, and I said that I had. There seemed to be some confusion as to who had gone, and I said that it was as if she felt I had left her. I reminded her she was the one who was gone. I also connected that maybe the feet were angry because she was gone. This type of interaction recurred in later sessions, until we discussed her anger more overtly, that the feet were hers and she would have to stop hurting me, when she did, and that she was the one who controlled the feet.

She continued some play with the schoolhouse, having the teacher punish one of the children. She would not answer me as to why the children were so bad. I then asked whether she wanted to go to school. She said when she's 4, but did not know when that would be. I told her when her birthday would be in January, and asked her whether she wanted to go to school then. She said no, and I said that she did not need to go then, but the law would say she had to go when she was 5 years old. I also told her she could change her mind about that and go a couple of days a week but that she could still come to see me on Fridays.

I brought in a book called *Billy and the New Baby* and read it to her. She loved the part about Billy being mad about the new baby and about his acting like a baby to get attention. We played cards and with dominoes and then, when there was not enough time to play with clay, she went to the dollhouse. She noted that the mother and father were in the playpen from the last time. I asked why they were in there, and she said, because they're acting like babies. I said, yes, like Billy, but reminded her that Billy decided it was more fun not to be a baby. She was particularly interested in the layette and weighing table. She put the dog on it and laughed and said she had a dog at home but did not know a name for it.

She demonstrated some sibling rivalry with anger at her father for bringing another child with him when visiting her and later expressed anger at a former patient by destroying a clay bell she had made and left with me. It was subsequent to this that her kicking me under the table escalated, and I set a limit on her hurting me. She didn't like my saying J. was angry, said the feet were angry, but finally admitted that they were her feet and that they were angry. She noted that I had put my feet to the side, so she couldn't kick me. I said yes, because it seemed that J's feet can't stop, and I hoped that she would learn to stop them—that it was hard to control them sometimes. She said, thoughtfully, with a sigh, yes. There was also a subsequent interaction with the grandmother in the living room around her wish to have a pair of scissors from her purse. Her grandmother had to take them away because she began brandishing them.

J. Jr. then went through a phase of being very good. This phase took the form of helping me clean up. It began when she noted that some paint brushes she had been using were hard. I said that they were hard and that we would have to wash them because the two girls who had used them had not done so. She thought that their parents should have had them wash them. I explained that I had not told on them. Later in the session, she said that I should have told on them and perhaps not have let them come back. I said that she thought I should have told on them, but I didn't, and that I would let them come back and would teach them. I also said that I would never not let her come back. At the end of this session, the longest cleaning-up session ensued that you could ever see. She was showing me how well she could clean up. We talked more about the girls' not cleaning up and that they shouldn't be allowed to come back. I had to reassure her again that I would have them come back but that I would teach them.

Her imperious and controlling style did not immediately disappear, however. In the next session, she ordered me around while working with wood, and while playing the matching game, she laughed in a gloating way when she was successful. I kept saying she could do it, and I knew she could do it. She began to tease me by mismatching cards and then played a game in which she covered up the correct space, and I tried to find it. She also informed me quite carefully that she was not going to school until she was 5 years old. There was also again some ordering me to pick cards up for her when they fell on the floor. At the end of the session, she began to tell me that her grandmother had told her there were robbers who steal things. She thought they hid in the bushes. I asked her whether she was worried for me. She said she was worried they would steal my money and said that I should hide it. I asked her where to hide it, and she said, in the closet where you keep the food.

In April, the termination phase may be said to have begun with a painting that J. Jr. initiated herself. She began to say that when she reached the H in the painting she would then leave. I told her that I would not see her the next week, unless granddad could bring her another night or day the following week. She said that she was wondering why she had to come now that B. is so nice and is letting her stay with granddad. I wondered whether that meant she was ready to stop coming. She said that she didn't know. I said I would have to talk with her grandparents but that she did not seem too sure about this now. Perhaps she thought that was the reason she was coming—about B. But now she was seeing me because she was so bossy and so angry at times.

In the following session, she again spotted the same goodbye drawing on the bulletin board. She asked again who had written goodbye on it. I said a little girl had who used to see me. And that we had talked about her saying goodbye sometime soon, in June. And that there was something I had to ask her—that her mother had called and wanted to know if she would mind her and her natural father visiting her this weekend. She said that it would be alright. She then told of her current concern—that her cousins had lost their newborn baby. There was a lot of trying to understand her in this, and then I asked her how she felt, she said "sad."

She continued her painting, after showing me a baby doll and bottle in her purse. The painting used all the colors and were lines; this changed into a game of finding my house, and then my finding her, and her finding me. So I talked of her worry that when we said goodbye she couldn't find me. I said she could always phone me—well, she had a phone, but it didn't work. So I said she could use granddad's; she asked me to put my phone number on the painting, which I did.

Following this, there was some re-emergence of the anger. It was expressed by dropping toys on the floor, which she imperiously commanded me to pick up, commanding me to put games away, and then by more overtly picking up the toy snake and hissing at me. She said the snake was angry at me that I thought she was angry at me. She said the snake was angry because I did not answer his question. I asked what the question was. She said: "What is your name?" I said my name and asked: "Who are you?" She could then turn to a more amiable play with the tea set, making a tea party. However, she again became angry when I wouldn't actually drink the water from the dirty teacups. I commented at this point that we had done all the things together that we had done over the months of our seeing each other—the giraffe game, the ring-toss game, and playing tea party—and that she would remember these when we were no longer seeing each other.

She wondered why she wouldn't be coming any more, and I said because she seemed to be doing okay now. She answered that, well, she was sometimes anxious. I asked what she was anxious about, and she said about B. I asked about that, and she said that she was still afraid that B. would come when her grandparents were not looking and take her away. I said they would never not be looking, and that seemed to be the end of that.

The next session, she told me that she had no more questions, only one: she was still worried about her friends' baby that died and whether they would be able to have another. But no more questions. I said that was why we would be stopping in June, because she had no more questions, but I would see her for one visit in July. She said that perhaps she wouldn't come in July and that I would be surprised and disappointed. I said she would be disappointing me because I was disappointing her by not seeing her after June. She got me sticky with clay and put a big fingerprint on the table as she asked me about where I worked. I continued that she was angry that I was disappointing her by not seeing her after June and that that was why she wanted to get me all sticky. I said I would see her next week and would then be away for 2 weeks for a vacation rest, but that I would send her a card. She then told me of her anger at grandad for withholding the card I had sent from my last trip and keeping it as his own. She was quite slow and perfectionistic again in cleaning up. Her grandfather told me that he had had to stop the car and administer a spanking because she had flicked his eye with a blanket while he was trying to drive. There was also a return of some foot kicking under the table in the following session. In close to the last session, the toy snake also hissed and bit at me. I said the snake was angry at me and went along with the game. I asked why, and she said, because it had asked me a question and I didn't answer. I said I didn't know the question, and she said she wouldn't tell me.

Her play with the schoolhouse concerned one child always being left out of the play, and she said it was because he was well. I asked why they left him out, and she said they didn't want him in their park. They kept kicking him off the equipment. She also had the boy hit the letters off the house, and all the children left school because it was "yukky" and they didn't want to come to that old school. I finally said that perhaps she wondered why I wouldn't be seeing her again. I told her that it was because she had had a worry about B. She said B. had no worries. I said she had had a worry about B. but that now she was safe with her grandparents, and now I had to see other children who had terrible worries. Would I see them on Friday nights? I said yes, and maybe on other nights as well. She began to put the letters away but then said that I should do it. I said she had played with them, she had to do it, but I would help. She said her grandma had always helped her. I had also said earlier that maybe she was angry because I wouldn't help her—that she wanted me to continue to help her.

During the termination session, she was somewhat demanding and somewhat provocative in the way she mixed the paints, and I had to set many limits. She took the snake and hissed at me. I hissed back and said the snake was angry, and I thought it was because it was the last time she was coming. At one point she denied this and said she was going to play with a toy next time, and I said that this was the last time. She agreed with a sigh that she was angry that she wasn't coming and that the snake was angry because I would not let her come back any more. She then settled down and continued to paint. We had a farewell dinner together. We also had a follow-up appointment with the grandparents and her. The grandparents reported that she had been quite aggressive and they felt that she believed she had lost her protection against B. taking her, when she stopped seeing me. Her mother reassured her that she was the one who had asked for her and that B. was asking for her because she had. Now she would not ask for her custody and she could remain with her grandparents as long as she wished. They believed that she was feeling more secure because recently, for the first time, she was able to sleep with the window open in the hot weather.

The case of J. Jr. is an example of a young child with severe separation-anxiety disorder. She was responding both to the earlier disruptions and to stresses in her life and to the current threat of losing the stability of the placement with the grandparents. Her symptoms were the intense fear and anxiety reaction related to the threat of parental loss as well as the rage related to the early deprivations. The reaction sometimes took the form of a behavioral disorder of aggression, controllingness, and demandingness. The neurotic core related to the feeling that she had done something wrong for which she was being punished: "Bad girl, bad girl." The early intervention allowed this child to continue on her own developmental track, with a good prognosis after the successful resolution of the custody battle.

The next case example is that of a boy first seen for a brief evaluation at age 6 and then for six sessions at age 8. Both contacts were at times of stress in the child's family environment. I hope to demonstrate the treatment of a relatively healthy child with neurotic symptoms that developed at a time of family stress. It might be interesting to demonstrate the use of a brief therapy model in the treatment of children.

The choice of brief therapy for a child needs to take

into account certain variables. One needs to assess the strengths in the family, both parents and child. One strength might be the intactness of the parental relationship but, as important, the level of family integration and development. Some of this can be assessed through history of how earlier conflicts were resolved. Most important is the capacity for the parents to support the treatment. The strength of the child can be assessed both through past history and by an initial evaluation.

The child strength one is looking for would include a sufficient level of object constancy and sense of self that enables the child to tolerate a brief relationship without too strong a reaction to termination of the relationship. The history would reveal that the child has had a normal healthy development prior to the present crisis, and the evaluation would rule out any more serious character or other pathology.

When there is sufficient strength in parent and child, and sufficient cooperation from parent and child, the other variable that is important for the choice of brief therapy is whether the situation presenting itself is of an acute or chronic nature. Characterological issues may be present with which the family is relatively satisfied, and they do not present with these. The present conflict is sufficiently separate that it can be resolved without too much attention to the character patterns of the child or family. An additional variable that one needs attend to in working briefly with a child is the reaction to separations. There needs to be sufficient toleration for interruptions and ability to handle transitions that a contact with a therapist for a brief time will not be reacted to as yet another stressor.

I see this type of intervention in three stages. In stage 1, one addresses the crisis directly with both parents and child, either separately or together. One may need to help them with the behavioral aspects of the crisis, that is, whatever child behavior itself that is causing the concern. The immediate tension needs to be drained, after which they can regroup and reorganize their forces. A further goal might be to help them learn to handle a crisis themselves, to plan for the future.

In stage 2, one can begin to help the family with the underlying issues. They may first need to be helped to see that the symptom presented is a cover for unresolved conflicts in the child and family. They can be redirected to understanding the underlying conflict. One may need to gather more information to help them further understand this conflict, at the same time that one gives the family more and more responsibility for this process.

In stage 3, simultaneous work with the child, the child is helped to master the symptom and begin to take responsibility early in the treatment process. The conflict is worked through at whatever level the child initially presents. The process is directed into a verbal symbolic mode when possible, and as soon as possible, so that cognitive processes, secondary process thinking, can take hold for the working through to be accomplished. Play can be useful in the initial stages of this process, or later, whenever repressions or resistances are experienced in the process.

Case Example: AL. AL's family was known to me prior to my seeing him for a brief evaluation at age 6. I had been asked to evaluate and then treat his 2 years older sister for behavior problems. During the course of this therapy relationship, the mother asked for a divorce from the father. I assisted the parents in planning a joint custody arrangement, where the children spent the week except for Wednesday night with the mother, and weekends with the father, at the original family home. The parents asked for a joint session with them and the two children to tell the children about the separation and planned divorce. They asked that I see AL to evaluate how he was taking the planned separation.

When I saw AL alone, he almost immediately said that everything was fine and that it was fine that his parents were separating. As he sat blocked, I suggested that he think of something to do. I described what was in the toy chest, and he continued to sit blocked for some time. I suggested either painting or drawing. He said he liked drawing, so I finally suggested drawing with crayons. He again sat and could not think of anything to draw. I started a variation of the Winnicott squiggle game. I started by drawing a hat, which he guessed immediately. Drawing 2 was his. I guessed a house, his father's house, and he then identified the figure he had drawn as his father. I asked how it would be to be away from that house, and he answered: "Then I won't have a swimming pool, I have to go in one bigger and deeper." He denied being scared by that. For my next turn, I drew a park (knowing there was one across the street from his mother's new apartment). He guessed a yard, and then the park at mother's apartment. He said he had visited it recently. His drawing, 4, I could not guess. I guessed a picnic, boxes, food, and he gave me a hint, something that goes in the wastebasket. I guessed garbage. I asked what was thrown away, and he said, "a pool." He said that he still might be happy when the pool might be thrown away, because we could go to the big swimming pool. Drawing 5 was mine. AL guessed correctly, "it's a swimming pool." Drawing 6 was AL's, a glass. I guessed this, but AL added that it was 7 Up, which I had given him. My drawing 7 was a cat (something his sister had been concerned about, who would get the cats). AL guessed our cat. His drawing 8 was a person smoking, and I guessed me or his parents smoking, and he said, just a person smoking. I drew number 9, and he guessed it's "me drinking 7 Up." AL's drawing 10 I guessed as someone smoking in bed, and AL said it was someone we didn't know, just because I wanted to. The figure was drawn on a bed that spelled bed. Here we began to talk of the different rooms people would be sleeping in, each of them having their own room, but mother would sleep on the floor. The cat never sleeps in her bed. The kittens do.

At the end of this session, I assessed that he was talking about his relationship with his father that was being thrown away. I felt that it was very deep, below the surface, accounting for the severe verbal blocking. At that time, I felt that he was handling the situation with denial. I wondered then whether there would be any advantage or possibility to bring this more into focus. It seemed to me that he would soon find out from the situation being lived out that he would be seeing his father about 4 days out of the week. "Recommendation: that the father continue to reassure him that he will see him much, is taking him on a trip...and will see him 4 days a week."

At age 8, AL was returned for a re-evaluation because he began having fears, particularly needing to follow his father around when he was in his father's house. During the 2 years between the initial session at age 6 and this current referral, his sister's treatment had been discontinued, and his father was being seen for once a week therapy. The sister had made some gains, after 2 years of treatment, and the father was having a depressive reaction to the dissolution of his marriage. He was expressing suicidal ideas at the time he referred his son for another evaluation.

I needed to make an assessment of his current strengths, and the relationship of the presenting symptoms to his father's condition. This would be necessary to evaluate whether he could be helped with a brief intervention or whether he would need longer treatment. Preferably, this would have been best with another therapist, since having therapy with more than one patient in the family can present major difficulties.

When I first saw AL again, he immediately remembered an Abraham Lincoln picture he had done for me 2 years before and said that he thought he had improved in drawing since then. I asked to tape record; after this was put on, he launched into a description of his fears. He proved to be extremely verbal at this time. He said that he was scared when he was alone in his room in the dark, but not when there were people around. Even though people were sleeping in the house with him, he was scared of the dark, but he was not scared in the day time. He said, though, that he was scared in the daytime at school when the girls talked of seeing faces on the washroom walls. I asked if he were scared if there was someone with him, and he said no. So we established that he was scared mostly when he was alone. But he said that he was also scared when he sleeps with father, and he sees his gray hair, and he thinks he will turn into a monster.

Then he told of a dream of mother that scared him. It emerged that he dreamed this when he was 6 years old—that something would happen to mother. She and he both fell off chairs. Then he remembered that Frankenstein put her in a bathtub and gave her a potion that made her very small and disappear. I said that he was afraid something would happen to mother. Yes, he said and then he would be all alone. I tried to link this to the divorce, by saying: "And we know what has been happening the last year and a half." He ignored this and went on to tell me of his sister's birthday party and the seance she had. He was looking forward to seeing Abraham Lincoln, whom he admired, but he was afraid that his eyes would be all sunken and his skin rotted and that he would be 7 feet tall. Then his father appeared, and he was frightened because he thought he was Abraham Lincoln. I wondered whether there was a connection, that he was afraid of father turning into a monster, and that something bad happened to Abraham Lincoln—he was shot. Then he truly would be all alone.

He also told of a scary story his sister told him about Dracula being below some stairs under his room, which he believed. I reintroduced the divorce. He insisted that all of this occurred before the divorce, that it started when he was six, that that was when he had the dream. Meanwhile I traced and summarized that he was afraid (1) when he was alone, (2) something would happen to his mother, (3) his father would become a monster, and (4) of seeing Abraham Lincoln—and his father came to the séance, and he was afraid of father.

I asked again whether it had anything to do with the divorce. He disavowed the feeling that it had, because it began when he was 6 years of age. He felt angry at the divorce and was afraid for awhile that he would be alone, but then the feeling disappeared. He was sure that it had nothing to do with the divorce. He said that his sister wanted him to steal mother's purse. He thought she had written a paper, and he wanted to find it and destroy it; the paper had the date of the divorce on it. I said that since it did not have anything to do with the divorce, it might take us some time to find out what the reason for the fears were, and we would have to see each other again. He went on to tell me how angry he got; he kicked in the door and broke a window. Father was never angry if he told the truth, but once he was a little angry. He really lost his temper. He felt that if he could only kick the monster, or really be angry at the monster, he would not feel afraid. I said that if he let his anger loose, maybe he wouldn't be afraid. Then he began to tell me that when his sister told him no one would get him because of his freckles, this made him feel better. Showing him a picture of Frankenstein made him afraid, talking about his fears made him afraid.

I said that what he wanted was someone to tell him that his fears were nonsense and that they would go away. I said that if I did that he might feel better for the moment, but that what he really needed was to find out the reasons that he felt afraid, so that they would go away for a long time. What I wanted was for him not to be bothered by these fears for all time—a little bit of a rash promise. He brought up his grandfather's death a month ago, and I related this to the fear something would also happen to father.

At the second therapy session, AL began by saying he did not want to come that day. I commented that he had hoped by coming once that his problems would go away. He countered by saying that he had told me everything. I reminded him of how long his sister had come. He was quite right in saying that different people had different problems. He did not know why his sister was coming. I said that was her business and that he was right that it might take a different problem a different amount of time. I then wondered whether what had happened to his grandfather, his dying, had something to do with his problem. (His father had had a strong grief reaction to this death.) He said that he was sad when his grandfather died, and he had cried, but that it happened 2 months ago, not 1 month ago. He said that it had been a month since he had been coming to see me. I said no, it was 2 weeks. He said he was afraid of monsters and that when he watched Frankenstein he had to sleep with his father for a week. His sister made him watch Frankenstein because she made fun of him for being scared. His sister made him do things. She got mad at him when he did not do what she wanted. I wondered why he had to do things for her. He said that she was the only one he had to play with. I wondered whether it was also important for him that she love him. He began to cry and, when I inquired why, he said that I had embarrassed him. I apologized for embarrassing him. After he settled down, I said that I was surprised, because I also had a brother and I had never been afraid to say that I liked him. He was surprised I had a brother, and he wondered whether we ever fought. I said yes, we used to, but that we had become really good friends. He wondered whether we had played together, and I said yes.

Then he began talking about having lost the high jump, and it emerged that the children had laughed at him—not when he missed the bar, but when he tripped afterward. He also said that he wanted to win that one because that was what he was really good at. When I said that he expected a lot of himself, he said that his mother said that too and that she really understood him. He went on to say that he was mad when they laughed, and then he laughed when they missed the bar. When his grandfather died, he was sad, not mad. He would have been mad if the doctors were on strike and if that was why he died—then he would have been mad and sad. But if he just died, then he would be sad. It was not clear whether he really believed that he died through lack of care or whether he was using this only as an example to differentiate between just being sad or being mad and sad at the same time. I told him at the end that I would see him on the tenth of the month, and we would see whether I needed to see him again.

AL began the third session by telling me a dream he had, a scary dream. He dreamed that he was in father's house, and a hand came up and grabbed his father. In talking about the dream, it emerged that what had frightened him was that something would happen to his dad and that then he would be all alone. He felt that he was the only one on his side, that everyone in the world except him was against him. In asking about this, it seemed that he felt that his sister was mean to him, that people, his mother and sister, were nice to him but that they turned mean; he could not count on them. I asked if he was ever angry, and he said yes—did he tell me the time that he kicked the door in? I said he had. He felt ashamed and embarrassed about this. He never told his sister that he was angry. I asked if he ever told his mother or father. Well, they knew when he's angry. He was sorry that he kicked the door in.

There was a pause, and I asked if he thought the arguments they had were somehow tied to his feeling that something might happen to his dad, and then he would be all alone. After much hesitation, he agreed that this might be so. I asked if it did have something to do with the divorce. He continued to insist that it does not. He stated that he was angry at mother, not at father, since it was mother who wanted the divorce, because of all the fights. I asked if he had felt that he lost the protection of his father because of the divorce. He said a little bit, but that he saw him on Wednesdays and weekends. I asked if he felt that his father should have fought to prevent the divorce, but I got little response from this.

We went over the above material a little. I told him of our next two appointments and of my 2 weeks absence. I asked him now how he had been feeling. He said that he had had this nightmare, but that he hadn't had them much before. I asked how it was when he was awake, and he said it had been much better. I commented that he was feeling better, and I would see him after my vacation for a checkup, that maybe it had helped to talk about things. He said he didn't know what had helped, that g-d was with him, and he always thought that the devil had had something to do with how he had been feeling. He was not ready to admit that what we talked about had helped much.

He then said that he had nothing more to talk about, although there were 20 minutes left in the 45-minute session. He felt that we had spent an hour. When I suggested drawing, he said that was not what he was supposed to do here. He then commented again on his drawing of Lincoln, criticized it, and commented on his sister's drawings on my bulletin board. Then he asked if I didn't see others. I said yes, but not all drew—some drew, some played with clay, some talked. I indicated that if he wanted, he could draw some time, that one could also talk and draw. He looked skeptical. But then he looked my whole office over, examining everything. Then he sat down and had me ask him hard questions about Abraham Lincoln, except when he was born.

He said he was thirsty and asked me, as he drank, what I did for fun with other people. When I said I painted, he asked to look at my paintings and said they should be in a museum. He told of a nursery school student who drew like a first grader. He saw the More cigarette ad on the bulletin board, and he had talked of my smoking and how much his grandpa had smoked. He told me of someone with a large collection of ads and then asked to look at my clavichord. At the end of the session, he said that the time had flown, that first he wanted to leave, and now he didn't want to leave—did I want to leave? I chuckled and said I had things to do, like washing the dishes.

I reminded AL of my vacation and when I would see him next. I said later, that if things continued to go as well as they had, that that might be the last time, unless his parents told me otherwise. He began almost immediately to tell me that he had had a bad dream, about Frankenstein. He was in the house with a lady, just some lady, and that Frankenstein came and grabbed him by the hand, and then his sister came and hit him with a broom stick. I related this dream to the one that he had had about father, that in that one also someone had him by the hand. He said that most of the fears were gone, just a little bit, just this much, measuring with his hands. He didn't know how, but he thought that maybe he expected me to help him, and just expecting me to help him made them go away, that he didn't care sometimes if he went to heaven. It would be fun, but it didn't matter what happened after you were dead. He mostly worried about monsters grabbing him. But now when he saw what he thought was a head in the pillows, he punched it in the face, and it went away.

Then he said that he really did not have much more to talk about. I said that it seemed as if most of it had gone, that sometimes when we have worries and we are able to talk about them, they seem less important and that they do go away. That next session we would see how it would be then, and if things continued to be going as well as they were, we could stop then.

He asked again for a drink of water, commented on my burned kitchen gloves, and asked me what I ate for dinner. Then he said again that he did not have much more to say. He asked if the tape recorder was still going. I asked if he'd like to listen to it. He thought that he sounded like a baby on it and asked me not to record. I turned it off but wondered if that was why he didn't want me to record—that I would like to record next time. He said that was alright. He just didn't want to listen to it, that he sounded funny on the tape recorder, much younger. Then he thought that he ought to see me four more times—had he seen me five times already? I said no, he'd seen me four times. I said again that we would see each other once more, and that might be the last time unless there was a reason to think things weren't continuing as well as they were now.

Then he did not know how to spend the last part of the session. He also suggested that it was confusing to change the sessions, and I said we could decide on a regular time if it were necessary to continue to see him. He chose a game to play, one he made up, in which each person wrote a number or letter and the other one completed it. Most of his at the beginning were faces, some of them looking much like Abraham Lincoln, and then later he did some birds and trees, after I had introduced ones like those.

The fifth session, 3 weeks later, was introduced again with AL saying that he had nothing to talk about that day. I said it was a checkup session to see how he was and to decide whether he should continue. He said that he wanted to be weller than well, like staying home from school an extra day. He said that he still feared a monster would get him in bed, no matter what side he slept on, that someone would come in the windows, and he was afraid when his father was not upstairs.

During this session, we explored his anger. Did he feel better when he let it out—or words. He said he felt better but he didn't think his fears had anything to do with his holding it in. He feared what he imagined, even though he knew they were not real. Usually he feared that something would happen to someone else, like being burned in the fire of the devil that he had imagined in the first place. He became afraid when father got angry, and threatened to do something, like put himself in the furnace or jump off a cliff when it looked like he was going to do it. His sister often believed he would and he would not. AL was able to say at this point that he got angry at his father and screamed at him, but he actively denied feeling guilty about it. Rather, he said that he felt relieved when he expressed the anger. I wondered after the session whether he was afraid of his father going out of control, and whether I should bring this out in the open.

We had an intermission during the session for me to give him a goodbye present, and we again looked at the designs on the bulletin board. He remarked on so many being his sister's—didn't I have other patients? I said yes, but we did other things. He asked about another child's present at this point, and he shared one with his sister that I had brought for her.

AL immediately said that he had nothing to say, in a final termination session. Again, it emerged now that he had told me what his fears were. I was supposed to tell him what to do to get rid of them. I explained that he did the work, by my helping him to understand where his fears came from, and then he would feel better—well, he did feel better after the last session, all the fears went away, so he did not think he had to come back.

I said that we could use this as a summary session to review what we had learned. Neither one of us got past his being afraid that something would happen to his father, so AL asked to listen to the tape of the previous session. We listened, but he claimed not to understand what his voice sounded like, although he could hear my voice. We stopped, and he had become agitated at the point where I asked him why he was afraid that something would happen to his dad. We were then able to reconstruct that what he was afraid of was his father's getting angry. We remembered his throwing or threatening to throw the cat's toys in the furnace, and the example of his saying not to go near the cliff, and then himself leaning over it (at a vacation spot). Then I wondered whether he hadn't also said he was afraid that his father had said he would throw the cats in the furnace. He kept saying that he only believed that this was what he was afraid of partially. I verbalized it more openly—that his father had felt badly about the divorce, and about his father dying, and maybe AL had been afraid he would do something to himself when he got so angry. Then AL would be left alone. He denied this and accepted it partially, but I felt finally that this was the crux of the matter. He had felt better after the last session because we had uncovered his fear of his father's anger.

I said then that the session was up, but that his father loved his children very much, showing him with my hands, and he would not do anything to leave them alone because of how much he cared for them. AL grinned broadly and showed by lengthening his hands that his father also got that angry. Then he put them on punishments, and maybe he punished himself as well, but he continued to grin very broadly.

We reversed the tape and then went out. AL asked me what I had wanted to be when I was his age, and I told him a librarian because I thought I would get to read all the books in the library. I asked him what he wanted to be. He wanted to be an artist. I told his mother that this was AL's last session. She said "Good work." He had also attributed the work to himself in the session. I said goodbye to mother and sister as well as to him and said we could make an appointment in the future, if needed. AL was afraid that now that he knew the sessions were over, thinking that would make the fears come back. I said no, that now he understood what he had really been afraid of. He told me now that he would tell his father to tell me the fears are all gone.

Follow-up information from his father revealed that the fears were largely resolved but occurred transitionally when his father argued with his sister. His improvement also dramatically paralleled his father's improvement in treatment. He had made a recent statement after an altercation with his father in the bathroom, "I'm tired of living," and his father saying, "I am so tired." At this time in the father's treatment, the suicidal ideas were resolving, and he was having a growing recognition that he was having histrionic outbursts similar to those displayed by his own father, when he was a child.

The work with the parents in this case was done primarily through the father's treatment. The decision for brief intervention with AL was made on the basis of his essentially healthy ego development, and his considerable intellectual, verbal, and symbolic capacities. It was felt also that this acute phobic crisis was in direct response to father's suicidal statements and that as the father improved, this stress would be resolved. A technical decision also had to be made not to deal with the normal oedipal aspects of the conflict, since in general he had been handling this well. He and his sister had also been handling the joint custody situation well, and initial problems in this had long ago been resolved through joint meetings between the mother and father.

This case also served as an example of the use of play during the largely verbal therapy, when there was blocking or resistance. Drawings were used in the initial evaluation, and later. AL made up a game of his own, when he was relieved of the feeling of guilt and could not talk. Although he did not focus on the usual play materials, he made much use of the environment to express himself. The bulletin board was an endless source of attention, as were other objects in the larger apartment.

10

DÉNOUEMENT AND TERMINATION

When to terminate a patient in treatment has been a much discussed issue since Freud's references to this subject in his *Collected Papers* (1953). The decision of when to terminate a child's treatment is often influenced by practical matters. The chid's course of treatment and its completion are often in the hands of the parents or guardian, who bring him to treatment. However, when a healthy alliance with the parents is achieved, the decision of when to terminate may be similar to that for treatments of other age groups.

When should psychotherapy be ended? Can we prevent future recurrence of symptoms for all time? In these days of brief therapy, the focus has been on the resolution of immediate and present crises, with the aim of placing the child on his own maturational and developmental track and the promise that all will be well; that is, other things being equal, there be no further stresses of a similar sort. Freud (1953) differentiated between chronic and traumatic precipitants to neurotic outbreaks. He indicated that the latter have the better prognosis, with the implication that these treatments may have a shorter course. Freud also demonstrated an understanding of the differential and lengthier response of character and more severe diagnoses to treatment.

How do we determine whether there is a favorable response during the course of treatment? What is the aim of a psychoanalytically oriented psychotherapy? When there is a pathological regression and an outbreak of symptom, whether it be characterological or neurotic, an assessment needs to be made as to whether it is related to an increase of impulse or a breakdown of ego controls. The increase of impulse in children or adolescents may be related to developmental phases such as puberty. The breakdown of ego controls may be related to developmental imperfections of either an organic or psychological developmental nature or increased chronic or traumatic stressors.

In the treatment of children and adolescents, one makes a decision within oneself and with the help of the parental guardians as to whether only the immediate crisis is to be treated or whether one is to go on to treat some of the earlier developmental arrests. When one chooses the latter course, treatment time is increased. The unconscious derivatives and memories of earlier developmental crises and conflicts have to be released, usually in a backward course over time. This process takes longer, and resistance against the pain of dealing with these earlier repressed memories may increase the time of treatment.

Normal and useful defenses may have become increased and rigid to deal with these painful memories and conflicts. Part of psychotherapy deals with the increased impulse life, allowing some dissipation of tension to make them easier to master. Much of psychotherapy deals with the rigid defenses and resistances to uncovering impulses and conflict to the time of developmental arrest and/or deviation.

It should not be expected that any psychotherapy will automatically innoculate the child or adolescent against all future psychological regressions. One hopes that, once the ego is strengthened, the child or adolescent can weather greater life stress. However, when developmental pushes of impulse are greater or if there is sufficient stress, there may be future need for return for prophylactic input or ego supportive care. When the patient, be he child, adolescent, or adult, has had a positive therapeutic alliance, these returns to treatment may be later positively sought and indeed asked for.

Two of my child cases returned to other therapists later at their own request. As I have often told my students, we only borrow these children from their parents—they don't belong to us. There should be no narcissistic injury if their return to treatment is with another therapist. They may have difficulty facing the embarrassment of what they now deem as having been a premature ending to treatment—their failure to use the treatment. They may not want to reawaken earlier separation anxieties, or their parents may displace their own resentments and anger: the "treatment was ineffective," "therapist was ineffective," "they only played." In a case in which I urged the mother to get intensive help for herself, the focus might have been on obtaining further help for the child with someone new who would at least initially buy her need to see only the child's issues and to "fix the child up."

A great deal can be done to strengthen the child and, in some family situations, this may be all that can be done. It is preferable if one can work with the family system and with the parents individually. Child and adolescent treatment are both slowed down and aided by this necessity. The extent of alliance bears an important influence on prognosis for the level of eventual therapeutic outcome as well as the length of treatment time. It also should be mentioned that length of treatment does not necessarily mean that the patient has been more disturbed. It might mean that more ambitious treatment was engaged in because of the anticipation of a more complete and healthy outcome.

The next question is when and how can we observe that the child or adolescent is on the right track toward resolution of conflict and is approaching a termination point? Freud (1953) emphasized the quantitative over the qualitative factor in making this determination. "In reality transitional and intermediate stages are far more common than sharply differentiated opposite stages... changes that take place are really only partial" (p. 330).

I have noted, however, in many of my treatments of children and adolescents, that there is a point or perhaps a phase that occurs that I have come to call the dénouement, or turning point, in the treatment. J., described in chapter 8, may be referred to as an example of this observation. J. was dealing with separation anxieties over my vacation and with a brief hospitalization and losses of grandmother and uncle. Note that my absences triggered concern backwards over these losses. The mother at about the same time discovered that she was not pregnant, and J. also explored and obtained information about birth. He also explored and remembered his previous therapist, whom he avowed he did not like as he experienced the separation anxieties.

The new stage in development is highlighted at the same time by his following up all these fears with the report that he had been able to stay up all night when he was sick and vomiting, without being afraid or calling his parents. "He used to be afraid that he would die when that used to happen." He also reported that he was less interested in superheros and more interested in real figures. At this point, his mother also came in to report not on how badly he was doing but on how *well* he was doing.

It was this stage that I called the dénouement or turning point in the treatment of J. Following Freud's description of phases rather than absolute points in time, however, this phase proved to be only one stage toward his eventual recovery. There was some regression, if one may remember from his account when his mother was rehospitalized.

One looks for three major indicators in the determination of this precursor to termination. One indicator is the report of major improvement in the home, reported by J.'s mother, and in the school setting. At this stage, J. was reporting children stealing his homework, a form of resistance to improvement. He was able to accept and use the therapist's suggestion that he lock his homework up in his locker. The second indicator would be resolution of symptom: gaining control over his fears of death, hence loss and separation anxieties. The third indicator would be evidence of developmental and maturational ego progress. J. moved from interest in superheroes and distanced fantasy to interest in reality: collection of coins and interest in real-life sports heroes, more age-appropriate indicators of ego development.

The treatment is by no means over at the turning point. The issues may need to be reviewed and worked over many times before termination actually occurs. The therapist, however, may now plan and look for the appropriate timing to suggest that termination be considered. I usually like to do this with the child first rather than have it come abruptly from the parent. You may have noted from the previous chapters that the signal comes from the child or adolescent that he is beginning to wonder how long this is going to go on. The patient may express it in the form of boredom with activities as they repeat the same theme or engage in the same activities over and over again. The signal may come from the patient in the form of a metaphor, concerning endings of something else in their lives.

This is the opening for which the therapist has been waiting. The therapist can now ask whether the child (or adolescent) has been thinking of when he would stop coming and how he would feel about it. This phase may take only 1 or 2 weeks, or much planning may have to take place for children with particular issues and stress about separations. I have had a child say she didn't need to come back at all. This can be a defense against experiencing the separation anxiety, so I usually insist that they come at least once more to say goodbye and also so I can prepare the parents. One child, who insisted that one session was all that was necessary, conveniently forgot to remind the parent that this was the last session, and the parent brought the child the following week at the regular time, when I was seeing another child for testing. The terminated patient had a broad grin on her face and enjoyed herself immensely during her usual session watching television while I tested the other patient. I had an opportunity for a follow-up with this particular child, when her stepbrother and stepsister were brought for help at a later time around some family stress. She was given an opportunity to ask for and explore any personal issues she might have remaining, but she said that she felt fine. She was a major support for these stepsiblings, who might previously have been perceived as a threat to her shaky feeling of security within the family.

For patients like J., a much slower course of termination often has to be planned. J. had a great feeling of comfort that the treatment had come to an end. He needed the reassurance that he would be seen again in several months for a checkup. These checkups are built into the termination process and are planned and dated visits. At the same time, the parents are given such a follow-up session to review progress and current events. I have reported on one family's attempt to move the treatment into family therapy as a resistance to separating from the therapist. They decided that they did not need family treatment once it was established that they would need to find a family therapist. I also allow telephone calls from both parents and patient around real or imagined crises. This can be a ploy and a resistance against ending—sometimes limits have to be set. In one case, the child was using the telephone calls to split me and the mother. I had to be quite firm in indicating to her repeatedly that her mother was responsible for her and that she would have to work things out with mother.

There can be other resistances to ending treatment. One well-known resistance is the return of previous symptomatology. Freud (1953) pointed out that once a decision is made to terminate, it is necessary to proceed with that plan. The symptomatic return has to be carefully explained in the case of children to parental figures so that they do not become alarmed and do not lose faith in the whole efficacy of the treatment: I brought my child to you for a cure, and he has the same problems. What have you been doing all this time, just playing?

This is a very difficult time for child patient, parents, and therapist.

This brings us to the therapist. The therapist can become very attached to the child/adolescent patient and have personal issues regarding separations. There is also the factor of conscientiousness, self-doubt about the effectiveness of the therapy, and perfectionism. Did I do enough? Should we have explored thus and so? One has to be quite aware of one's own blind spots and issues in doing any type of counseling or therapy (Freud, 1953). Freud recommended frequent reanalysis for analysts. We encourage self-exploration and personal treatment on a volunteer basis for our students in clinical and counseling psychology. Complete reconstruction may be an admirable goal but is seldom achieved. Time, energy, and finances are not infinite. Remember, we only borrow these children—they belong to their parents.

REFERENCES

Aoki, S. (1981). The retest reliability of the Sand Play Technique. II. *British Journal of Projective Psychology and Personality Study, 26*, 25–33.

Axeline, V. (1947). *Play therapy*. New York: Houghton-Mifflin.

Bach, G. R. (1945). Young children's play fantasies. *Psychology Monographs, 59*, (2, Whole No. 272).

Beiser, H. (1976). Play equipment. In C. Schaeffer (Ed.), *Therapeutic use of child's play* (pp. 423–435). New York: Jason Aronson.

Blatt, S. J. (1975). The validity of projective techniques and their clinical and research contributions. *Journal of Personality Assessment, 39*, 327–343.

Buhler, C., & Kelley, G. (1949). *The world test. A measurement of emotional disturbance*. New York: Psychological Corp., 1941.

DesLauriers, A. M., & Carlson, C. F. (1969). *Your child is asleep*. Homewood, IL: Dorsey Press.

Ekstein, Rudolph (1966). *Children of time and space of action and impulse. Clinical studies on the psychoanalytic treatment of severely disturbed children*. New York: Appleton-Century-Crofts.

Erikson, E. H. (1964). Clinical observation of play disruption in young children. In M. R. Haworth (Ed), *Child psychotherapy* (pp. 264–277). New York: Basic Books.

Esman, E. H. (1983). Psychoanalytic play therapy. In C. E. Schaefer & K. J. O'Connor (Eds.), *Handbook of play therapy* (pp. 11–21). New York: John Wiley & Sons.

Field, T., De Stefano, L., & Koewler, J. H. III (1982). Fantasy play of toddlers and preschoolers. *Developmental Psychology, 18*, 503–508.

Freud, A. (1947). *The psychoanalytic treatment of children*. London: Imago Publishing.

Freud, S. (1953). Analysis terminable and interminable (1937). In *Collected papers* (Vol. V). London: The Hogarth Press Ltd and The Institute of Psycho-Analysis, pp. 316–357.

Gewirtz, J. L. (1950). An investigation of aggressive behavior in the doll play of young Sac and Fox Indian children and a comparison to the aggression of midwestern white preschool children. *American Psychologist, 5*, 294–295 (abst).

Gondor, L. H. (1964). Use of fantasy communications in child psychotherapy. In M. R. Haworth (Ed.), *Child psychotherapy* (pp. 374–383). New York: Basic Books.

Howe, P. A., & Silvern, E. (1981). Behavioral observation of children during play therapy: Preliminary development of a research instrument. *Journal of Personality Assessment, 45*, 168–183.

Jeffre-Isch, M. (1952). Fantasied mother–child interaction in doll play. *Journal of Genetic Psychology, 81*, 233–258.

Jernberg, A. M. (1979). *Theraplay*. San Francisco, CA: Jossey-Bass.

Klein, M. (1948). *Contributions to psychoanalysis, 1921–1945*. London: Hogarth.

Klein, M. (1964). The psychoanalytic play technique. In M. R. Haworth (Ed.), *Child psychotherapy* (pp. 277–287). New York: Basic Books.

Kohut, H. (1983). *Analysis of the self. Monograph series of the psychoanalytic study of the child*, No. 4. New York: International Universities Press.

Kozloff, M. A. (1973). *Reaching the autistic child: A parent training program*. Champaign, IL: Research Press.

Krall, V. (1953). Personality characteristics of accident-repeating children. *Journal of Abnormal and Social Psychology, 48*, 99–107.

Krall, V., & Irvin, F. S. (1973). Modalities of treatment in adolescence. *Psychotherapy, Theory, Research and Practice, 10*, 248–250.

Lerner, E., & Murphy, L. B. (Eds.) (1941). Methods for the study of personality in young children. *Monographs of the Society for Research in Child Development, 6*, (4, Whole No. 30).

Levy, D. M. (1937). Studies in sibling rivalry. *Research Monographs. American Orthopsychiatry Association*, (2, Whole No. 2).

Lowe, D. M., & Costello, H. (1976). *Manual for the Symbolic Play Test*. Windsor, England: NFER.

Lowenfeld, M. (1970). *The Lowenfeld technique*. Oxford: Pergamon Press.

Mahler, M. (1967). *The psychological birth of the human infant*. New York: Basic Books.

McLoyd, V. C. (1983). The effects of structure of play objects on the pretend play of low-income preschool children. *Child Development, 54*, 626–635.

Miller, W. T. (1982). Cross-over therapy with children and adolescents. *Topeka State Hospital Collected Papers, Reunion of 1982, Topeka, Kansas*.

Murphy, L. B. (1956). Personality in young children. I. Methods for the study of personality in young children. New York: Basic Books.

Pelligrini, A. B. (1982). Interpreting children's play. *Journal of Children in Contemporary Society, 14*, 47–58.

Phillips, R. (1945). Doll play as a function of the realism of the materials and the length of the experimental session. *Child Development, 16*, 123–143.

Piaget, J. (1962). *Play, dreams and imitation in childhood*. New York: W. W. Norton.

Pintler, M. H. (1945). Doll play as a function of experimenter–child interaction and initial organization of materials. *Child Development, 16*, 145–166.

Pulaski, M. A. (1976). Play symbolism in cognitive development. In C. E. Schaefer (Ed.), *Therapeutic use of child's play* (pp. 27–43). New York: Jason Aronson.

Robinson, E. F. (1946). Doll play as a function of the doll family constellation. *Child Development, 17*, 99–119.

Sarnoff, C. (1976). *Latency*. New York: Jason Aronson.

Sears, P. S. (1951). Doll play aggression in normal young children: Influence of sex, age, sibling status, father's absence. *Psychology Monograph, 65*, (6, Whole No. 323).

Sjolund, M. (1981). Play-diagnosis and therapy in Sweden: The Erica method. *Journal of Clinical Psychology, 37*, 322–325.

Udwin, O. A., & Yule, W. (1982). Validation data on Lowe and Costello's Symbolic Play Test. *Child Care, Health and Development, 8*, 361–366.

Walder, R. (1976). Psychoanalytic theory of play. In C. E. Schaefer (Ed.), *Therapeutic use of child's play* (pp. 79–95). New York: Jason Aronson.

Winnicott, D. W. (1971). *Therapeutic consultations in child psychiatry*. New York: Basic Books.

INDEX

ABOUT THE AUTHOR

Vita Krall, Ph.D., obtained her bachelor's degree from Antioch College in 1944, her master's degree from the University of Iowa in 1945, and her doctorate in Clinical Psychology from the University of Rochester in 1951. She holds a Diploma in Clinical Psychology from the American Board of Professional Psychology, and was honored by the same in 1987 with a Distinguished Service Award. In 1983, Dr. Krall was named Distinguished Psychologist by the Illinois Psychological Association.

Dr. Krall began her practical clinical training with a rotating internship in the state of New York from 1945–1947. She then was an instructor in the Department of Psychology at Michigan State University, senior clinical psychologist at the Topeka State Hospital, acting director of psychology at the Kansas Neurological Institute, and staff psychologist at the Child Guidance Clinic of Greater Bridgeport, in Bridgeport, Connecticut. From 1963–1989, Dr. Krall worked at the Institute for Psychosomatic and Psychiatric Training at the Michael Reese Hospital and Medical Center in Chicago, first as senior clinical psychologist and later as chief child psychologist and director of training in clinical psychology.

Dr. Krall is presently director of a research project studying Crohn's disease in children at Hartford Hospital, in Hartford, Connecticut.